LAURA KOMÓCSIN PCC

50

Secret Coaching
Stories from the Top

LAURA KOMÓCSIN PCC

50

Secret Coaching
Stories from the Top

Business Coach
Budapest, 2016

Author: Laura Komócsin PCC
Editor: Anikó Uj
Translator: Lívia Gecse
Layout: Imre Arany
Graphics: Édua Szűcs

CONTENTS

CHAPTER 3

The Little Match Girl

CHAPTER 4

The Snow Queen

CHAPTER 5

The Princess and the Pea

CHAPTER 6

The Ugly Duckling

CHAPTER 7

The Little Mermaid

CHAPTER 8

The Steadfast Tin Soldier

INTRODUCTION

Since this is a storybook, let me start it with the story of how I became a coach.

Between 1998 and 2004, I worked as a management consultant for Accenture, a global consulting and technology firm. In 2004, my daughter Izabella was born. She was six weeks old when a director of a large bank called me on the phone:

– Laura, I would like you to come to work for us. This project we're running is just cut out for you. I know how well you manage teams, and I think you would do a great job on this project as well.

– Well, you know, my daughter is just about six weeks old, I'm not in a position to start a more-than-full-time job right now.

– I'm sorry to hear that.

Two weeks passed. My phone rang again:

– I've thought it through. If we put some really strong sub-team leaders reporting to you, you could manage this project with six-hour workdays.

– I do appreciate it that you insist on my being part of your project. But look, my daughter is just eight weeks old. She really needs me by her side.

He called me again two weeks later:

– We have a young, high-potential project manager candidate. If you two split the role, you could each do a four-hour shift every day.

– But Izabella is still only ten weeks old…

– Well, how many hours do you want to work, then????

– Two hours PER WEEK.

He just laughed…

Another two weeks passed…

– When you said you wanted to work two hours per week, I thought you were joking. But then I had this idea: we could put the young high-flier in charge of the whole project, and you could come in to coach him two hours per week. How does that sound to you now?

I said:

– Sounds great! I have one concern, though: I did learn something about coaching in the U.S., but I've never actually done it myself. It's important for us to have a "win-win" situation. Why don't we make an agreement? I'll coach him for free for six months. You give me feedback on how I'm doing as we go along, and at the end, you give me a letter of reference. Afterwards, if you decide to do so, we can go on with the coaching on a commercial basis.

That's how we did it. After six months, we signed a contract that suited us both. My daughter still had a full-time mother, and I could go back to work – in fact, I had just found a new career for myself!

When my second child, Ágoston, was born, I had another big decision to make: over the two years or so before his birth, I had gathered so many coaching clients, I was working almost 40 hours per week again. I wanted to give him the same attention and care as I had given to my daughter. However, I did not want to continue working full time – on my own. So I decided to build a team.

Coaching is a profession based on a very high level of trust. You don't search for a coach in the Yellow Pages. So I started training future coaches, sharing my lessons learned, and selected the best of them to be part of my team. I could see how they worked and feel assured that they would share my professional values. Today, I continue to both coach and train the new generation of coaches together with key members of my team in order to be able to give my full attention to my grandchildren when they are born…

I started coaching executives in 2004, and I have been training new coaches since 2007. During the coach training sessions, I always share my professional experiences so that the next generation will not make the same mistakes that I made. I also often share coaching stories that are educational as well as entertaining. These stories ended up in a volume published in Hungarian in 2012. Since then, however, I have accumulated so many more coaching stories about international (meaning, non-Hungarian) executives that the time seems to have arrived to publish them in another book, this time in English, for an international audience. Among the top managers I have coached in this context have been a Brazilian executive who did not understand what work-related stress means, a director from South Korea who sacrificed her marriage and her children for the sake of her career and a Canadian top executive who decided to go down the opposite path, as well as an American man who commuted to work by helicopter every day. And many others. Each of these was a person of a different age and nationality working in a different industry, but they all had something in common: they were all seeking a coach in order to become happier and more successful.

As the founding president of the Hungarian Chapter of the International Coach Federation, I have always considered the sharing of coaching skills to be my duty, and I believe this book (published in both Hungarian and English) will serve as the best means to decrease the professional "mystification" of coaching and to help new coaches, who all work with a certain degree of uncertainty, by sharing the experiences of some "old hands", and also by showing potential customers how effective coaching can be.

For confidentiality reasons, the identities and personal information of the coachees cannot be disclosed, so their names, positions, and industries have been altered to protect their identity.

My first book[1] contained 150 coaching tools accompanied by several anecdotes. Most of my earlier clients – whose stories were described in the book – received a complimentary edition along with instructions to let me know if they were able to recognize themselves in my stories. I was also curious to see if they would recognize themselves, since I had written their stories by altering their personalities and circumstances. In the following few weeks, I received many text messages and emails saying: *Yes, we got it.*

There was one executive, however, who did call me, and he was quite upset about not finding his story in the book.

I had promised that his story would be published, but he thought that it hadn't been! I quickly grabbed the book and told him which page to look up. He quietly read the story while I remained on the line. Then he told me that he wasn't upset any more about excluding him from the book. What he was upset about now was that the story was not true, that I had exaggerated too much. I replied that I had exaggerated in his own interest, and for the sake of amusing my readers.

He started fuming again. "What? My story wasn't interesting enough? You think that I am a *nobody*?"

At this point, I started to lose my patience and felt that the proper thing to say was, "No, I don't think you

---

1 Laura Komocsin: *Toolful Coach: SPARKLE coaching model with 150 useful tools and case studies*, Amazon, 2012

are a *nobody*, but based on your previous three sentences you seem to tend to take things way too personally. If you'd like to talk about this, I can refer you to a great psychologist."

So what's the conclusion here? Many people are happy to see their story in a book. Others do not recognize themselves, because their sense of self-awareness is not strong enough. In this book I have tried to find the right balance between telling true stories and giving the "extra touch" only when absolutely necessary.

I found further inspiration from Rolf Wunderer, who uses fairy tales from the Grimm brothers in order to give the right meaning to his management training. He believes that stories both help to bring to the surface the creative and curious inner child inside a person and allow everyone to think more freely: free of pre-conceptions and conventions. At the same time, fairy tale characters are often exaggerated, and the stories' relevance becomes more obvious through the archetypal behaviors they contain. In his book Aesop and the CEO[2], David Noonan came to the same conclusion that the Iranian-German psychiatrist Nossrat Peseschkian did in his[3]. We tend to remember symbolic messages from a fairy tale far better than we do pure theories and

2 David C. Noonan: *Aesop and the CEO: Powerful Business Insights from Aesop's Ancient Fables,* Thomas Nelson, 2005
3 Nossrat Peseschkian: *In Search of Meaning: Positive Psychotherapy Step by Step Springer Verlag Berlin Heidelberg New York Tokyo*

concepts. My own first book[4] turned out to be a bit dry, so I thought it was time to leverage it with a new publication – and also because I have realized that most executives only read the case studies anyway.

Just as Rolf Wunderer relied on the Grimms, David Noonan on Aesop, and Nossrat Peseschkian on tales from the Middle East, I originally considered using the Collection of 77 Hungarian Folk Tales as the framework for my new book. However, since Hungarian folk tales are not well known internationally, and having the intent of publishing my book in English, I also started to think about another context. Finally, I settled on Hans Christian Andersen, the Danish author whose fairy tales have been translated into more than 125 languages and are today known worldwide.

I listened to and watched many Andersen tales as a child, and every single time I cried when the Little Match Girl died and always worried about the little boy who told the Emperor that he was not wearing anything at all. As a teenager, I sometimes felt like an Ugly Duckling (a story Andersen meant to be auto-biographical), and when I first fell in love, I wondered what I would have done if I had been the Little Mermaid. Whenever I met perfectionists similar to that in the tale of the Princess and the Pea, my childhood bedtime

---

4   Laura Komocsin: *Toolful Coach: SPARKLE coaching model with 150 useful tools and case studies,* Amazon, 2012

stories often came to my mind. In some regards, Andersen has been around me all my life. I have visited Denmark, the homeland of Andersen, several times, both as a child and also as an adult with my children. And the fact that my first employer was Andersen Consulting (now Accenture) seems like a   pretty significant coincidence to me.

So I decided that even if couldn't use all of 156 of Andersen's tales in this volume, I could at least use the most widely known ones to serve as the overall theme for individual chapters.

- *Once upon a time…* this chapter contains stories about the beginning of the coach-coachee relationship, how they get involved in the coaching process, and factors that influence the coachee when choosing the right coach.

- In the story *The Emperor's New Clothes*, two weavers promise an emperor a new suit of clothes that is invisible to those who are unfit for their positions because they are stupid or incompetent. When the Emperor parades around before his subjects in his new clothes, no one dares to say that they don't see the new garments until a child cries out, "But he is not wearing anything at all!" This chapter of the book contains stories in which the coach highlights points that the executive did not realize, or was not aware of, and was surprised by the discovery. Other stories describe executives trying to exaggerate and put on a show for others, while others involve suspicions of a lie, corruption or other unacceptable practices.

- In Andersen's tale of the same name, *The Little Match Girl* is out in the cold night on New Year's Eve, in torn clothing, without shoes, selling matches from her apron. But nobody wants to buy them. Almost frozen, she starts warming her hands by lighting the matches one by one. In the light of every single flame she experiences a vision of herself happily feasting together with her long-dead grandmother, whose presence she has long yearned for. She has seen the light – and by the next morning she has left this dark world. The chapter entitled the "Little Match Girl" relates to stories about poverty and times when small joys bring great happiness.

- *The Snow Queen* is about strong personal relationships and solitude that lack the experience of being loved. The Snow Queen lived in her gorgeous white empire, all covered by snow and ice, far away in the North. It was not only her empire that was made of ice: her heart was as well. She had a special "troll mirror" whose reflection turned everything into the opposite of what it was: everything that was nice appeared to be ugly, and even the smallest mistake was exaggerated into a huge one. One day, however, the mirror shattered, and all the small pieces were scattered all over the world. Every little piece of the shattered mirror exerted the same negative effect as the original one: if one of them got into someone's eye or heart, the person would instantly turn into a cold and mean creature. Later, Gerda and Kay, two poor children living next door to each other, learn about the power of the shattered shards when some of them get into Kay's heart and eye, making him turn cruel and aggressive. Gerda does her best to free him from the evil spell, and after many adventures in the Snow Queen's land, they return to Kay's grandmother and live happily ever after. This chapter of the book deals with stories about loud, aggressive, control-freak executives and situations involving severe conflicts.

- In *The Princess and the Pea*, a young prince wants to marry a princess who was born to be a queen. He searches the whole world to find the right one – with no luck. One night, in the middle of a huge storm, somebody knocks on the door, and there is a princess, soaking wet, asking for shelter. The old king and his wife decide to put the princess to a test: they place a single pea underneath her mattress in order to see if she will notice it. In the morning, the princess complains about not being able to sleep due to the mattress being uncomfortable. The prince is happy because he has finally found his true mate: it could only be a princess who would be so particular about her comfort. The prince marries her right away, and the pea is put into the treasury. For this chapter of the book, I gathered stories about perfectionist executives and situations in which a tiny little thing served as the distinction between decisiveness and uncertainty.

- *The Ugly Duckling* is a fable about a mother duck who has laid her eggs, and all but the largest one have hatched. The mother duck is worried, so she continues incubating the remaining egg. Finally, when the egg hatches, the little duckling that emerges proves to be very ugly, so all the other ducks make fun of him. He is often hurt by his peers, who don't like him, so he decides to go out into the world, where he has many adventures and painful experiences. In the meantime, he grows up to be an adult. One day, he sees swans flying in the air, and the swans land on the water where he is swimming. He sees his own image in the water and realizes that he looks the same as the swans. The swans accept him, and from that moment on he lives happily ever after. The stories in this chapter are about change, about people not being happy where they are, and most importantly, finding their true self as a result of their adventures.

- *The Little Mermaid* is a story about the widowed Sea King and his six daughters, who all lived deep under the sea. The youngest daughter was the prettiest one. She was very interested in the world of humans. The girls were only allowed to see the outside world once they reached their 15th birthday. Each time when her five elder sisters returned, they all told a different story about it. When her turn came, the youngest got involved with a young prince. She got to know him, and even saved his life, but the prince could not return the favor. The little mermaid paid a high price for getting to know the outside world, and did everything for her love, even at the cost of her own life. This chapter contains stories about the importance of being a woman: the woman as a seductress, as a mother and in many other roles.

- The tale of *The Steadfast Tin Soldier* is about a boy who gets 25 tin soldiers for his birthday. One of them has only one leg, but stands just as sturdily as his brothers. The tin soldier's life changes when he discovers a paper castle inhabited by a ballerina who also stands only on one leg while holding the other up in the air. He falls in love with the ballerina. One day, the tin soldier is placed on the windowsill and, blown away by the wind in a storm, falls to the ground. After many adventures, he finds his way back to the ballerina. But only for a short time before they are engulfed in flames in the fireplace. For this chapter of the book, I gathered stories about resilience and when having a courageous heart played the most important role.

The protagonists in this book are my coachees from the corporate world: managers, executives, directors, CEOs... and professionals with many other titles too. I selected 50 of my coaching stories for this book, so I hope this book will be useful for not only (my) coachees and coach trainees, but for anyone anywhere in the world who would like to take a peek into the secret life of corporate top dogs through the eyes of an executive coach.

And why is this book illustrated with caricatures? The word "caricature" is derived from the Italian "caricare" – to exaggerate or load. In literature, a caricature is a description of a person that exaggerates some characteristics and oversimplifies others.[5] We coaches do something similar to what caricaturists do by showing a distorted mirror to our clients, sometimes exaggerating things in order to convince them to find greater motivation to change. It was this parallel that inspired me to ask the well-known Hungarian caricaturist Édua Szűts to complement my book with her drawings.

I hope you enjoy reading it!

Laura Komócsin PCC

5   en.wikipedia.org/wiki/Caricature

CHAPTER 1

Once Upon a Time...

1

THE KNIGHT WHO WAITED FIVE YEARS FOR THE SLEEPING BEAUTY

It is common knowledge that the success of a coaching process largely depends on the goal setting. In the corporate world, personal development objectives often originate from the result of 360 degree assessments or other forms of feedback gathered from colleagues or other observers. The typical reactions to such inputs can be sorted into three categories.

The first category is when the coachee just waves his hands and says, "They have got it all wrong."

This may well be true: maybe a specific behavior occurred only once when the coachee was in a bad mood, and he doesn't usually behave that way. Or, it may be the classical example of denial, when you know all too well that you have to improve in a certain aspect, but you refuse to admit it to yourself.

The second category of reactions sounds like this:

"They are right. That is how I really am, I do behave like that, but it is not on my list of priorities right now to change this." This can also be a very human reaction. There are times when you are not good at something, you do accept that this is not good for the others but you have more important things in focus at the moment.

And here comes the third type of reactions, which lead us to a real coaching objective:

"They are right. This also bothers me a lot, and I do want to change this."

Besides setting the goal for the coaching process, the other important success factor is the existence of chemistry between the coach and the coachee, meaning the degree to which an executive can trust and open up to the coach during the interaction.

Some time ago, a daily newspaper published an interview with me. A deputy CEO of a large company read the article and decided that either I would be his coach or nobody would. He told his CEO about this, and since the CEO wanted to get to know me personally as well, we had lunch together and discussed the process. Then he gave his approval. Time passed, but no purchase order was sent by the HR department of the company. It turned out that as long as the HR manager was there, there wasn't going to be an order at all. In the meantime, the CEO was relocated to another country and was replaced by someone else. I also talked to this new CEO, who also gave his approval – but again, the HR manager vetoed the process and suggested three other coaches to be considered by my future client deputy CEO. The answer was the same as before: either me or nobody. As I had only talked to the CEOs up to that point, we still hadn't met personally, but he became increasingly motivated to stick up for his decision. Then the second CEO also moved to another country, and my future client was promoted to the position – so we finally had a chance to meet.

At this very first meeting, he told me about all the things he had done for this encounter to finally happen. I had mixed feelings about it: I felt honored, happy, proud, but also a load of weight, responsibility and stress… but looking back, I feel that this was the easiest coaching process of my life. My simple presence was quite sufficient. I am convinced that even if I had done something wrong, the client would still have been satisfied, because he wanted this coaching process so badly, and it was really important to him – which meant that he actually coached himself during the process, I only provided a framework for it. I respect him as a wise and mature leader who really needed only this much.

2

HOMEMADE PLAY DOUGH

In his bestseller book *Everything I Need to Know About Being a Manager, I Learned from My Kids*[6] Ian Durston lists all the skills needed to succeed both at work and at home. I thoroughly enjoyed reading the book myself, but felt one topic was missing: if you learn to make homemade play dough, you'll stand a better chance of being selected as a CEO's coach. As Durston did not include this in his book, I add this story to my own.

My personal reason for career change was to spend more time with my kids than I could when I was working as a consultant at a multinational company, flying between Budapest, Amsterdam and Kuala Lumpur. I also learn a lot from my kids looking at things from a different perspective, but I had never thought that one day they would help me to win a coaching assignment.

For a coach, credibility is paramount – maybe even more so than for other professions. You can easily question a coach's credibility if the coach offers

---

6   Ian Durston *Everything I Need to Know About Being a Manager, I Learned from My Kids*. Piatkus, 2009.

support in time management, but is late for your first appointment. Or if the coach promotes services in sales coaching, but lacks a list of client credentials. Or if the coach specializes in strengthening self-confidence, but then apologizes incessantly for every little thing.

A CEO was looking for a coach to help him with work-life balance. His HR manager put forward a long list of highly qualified coaches, from which he was unable to pick out one based solely on professional background. The CEO, who had a five-year-old son, finally made a shortlist of three coaches – all married with young children. He met the three coaches and asked a simple question: "Could you tell me the recipe for how to make play dough at home?" Those who could not answer lost their credibility. The CEO found it hard to believe that their own work-life balance was working.

As my daughter was about the same age as the CEO's son, playing with homemade play dough was not unusual in my own household. After my answer to his question, the CEO picked me as his coach – not because I am highly skilled at handicrafts.

During our coaching process the play dough came to play a role one more time. The same CEO was complaining that he was wasting a lot of time trying to resolve conflicts between his directors.

A few days earlier, I had bought a 12-color play dough set for my daughter. She was playing happily in the kitchen when her younger brother appeared and wanted to join in. She got possessive, threw a tantrum, and within seconds I had two screaming kids on my hands. As a wise mother who knows how to handle such conflicts – and knows everything else, in fact – I intervened: I made two piles of dough, each made up of six different colors, and told them to play with one pile each. I thought I could leave them alone now, but they continued to scream at each other. I had no idea what the matter was but I started to lose my patience so I said to them: "Okay, now you two have exactly one minute to sort out your problem yourselves. If you can't, then I will take away all the dough and send you both to your rooms."

Then they shut up and pushed both piles of dough to the center of the kitchen table. One of them started to roll a piece, the other used a cookie cutter to cut out shapes. It turned out they hadn't been arguing about the colors, it was just that they wanted to play with the dough in different ways.

End of story. Its moral – both for my kids and my CEO client: do not use your authority to resolve conflicts between your kids/colleagues. Use empowerment instead.

3

LOOKING FOR BUGS
IN MY OFFICE

Coaching sessions typically take place in three different environmental settings. The first one is the classic scenario: the coach goes to meet the coachee in his/her office. There are advantages to this, being time-efficient for the coachee, parking is also available for the coach in most cases, and the most important being that the coach can always get some insight into the coachee's working environment. Spending one hour there usually tells you a lot. How many times was he interrupted during the session, by whom and for what reason? How did he behave with the "intruders"? What does his office look like compared to the others'? But you can also discover some interesting things about the coachee while taking the elevator upstairs to the office…

On one occasion, an executive with an office on the top floor of the building was seeking a coach for himself. His secretary came down to meet me at the reception downstairs, and after the other passengers left the elevator, I asked her what she thought about her boss. "He's cute!" she answered, without hesitation. Her face blushed slightly as we left the elevator, and we both laughed. She eased my stress before the first encounter, and she became a really good assistant to the coaching process as well.

Since our first (preliminary) meeting was in his office and he had selected me to be his coach, I invited him to the first working session in my own office. When he arrived, he didn't even take his coat off but immediately started looking around my office. He looked behind the curtain, underneath the coffee table, looked through the books on the shelves. I was completely surprised and after a while I asked him what he was searching for. "Bugs," he answered without hesitation. I know it may seem like I am only writing this to create a story, but honestly, at first I really thought he was looking for a real, living bug, like a cockroach or an ant. But before I could turn my head, he explained that he is the vice president of a large company listed on the stock exchange, and anything he says could have an effect on the stock price, so he had to be especially careful. Since I had no experience with such situations, I immediately offered to hold the coaching session at another place if he thought the office might be bugged. Finally we went over to a coffee shop, where he seemed to get a bit more relaxed – until he asked me to remove the batteries from my phone.

This was the point when I ran out of my stock of empathy and consideration and I decided I was not the right coach for him. I said this to the executive, who replied that he had just been testing me, and my courage had convinced him that I was the right coach for him.

FRIENDSHIP OR LOYALTY?

Many CEOs have no problems with delegation, motivation or time management. They seek coaching support with various leadership dilemmas. Often it is a clash of values: the owner of the company may want higher profits, while the CEO has environmental or social responsibility concerns more at heart.

The CEO of a 2,000-employee company called me once. He was in his forties, but was dressed like a hippie, not like a CEO. His dilemma was one of choosing either friendship or loyalty to the owners. Obviously, the coach would never make the choice for him but could help him make up his own mind.

We used the SPARKLE coaching model[7] and started the process of understanding the situation. The problem was an ethical one: the CEO had learned that his best friend, who was also a direct report to him, had been involved in corruption. The CEO explained he was unsure what he should do. On one hand, he felt somewhat sympathetic

---

7   To read more about the SPARKLE coaching model, see the book *Toolful Coach* by the author.

toward his friend: a father of five, with no college degree, and therefore a relatively low salary.

The CEO also explained that he felt stressed every day by the time he got to work: although he had a company car, his wife drove it, and he used public transportation to get to his office – without a valid ticket. He was angry with the public transportation company and he refused to buy a ticket. Because of this, he was constantly under stress over the possibility of being caught for fare evasion.

In truth, he did not want a coach to support him in making the correct decision – even if this was what he had said – because he had already made the decision. He only wanted to get "approval" of his decision – so he hadn't been honest with me, either.

I declined to be his coach. Instead, I mailed him a copy of the October 2009 edition of the Harvard Business Review, which covered business ethics at great lengths, under the title Honesty, Trust, Reputation.

5

WHO PAYS THE BILL?

My coaching company is the market leader in Hungary, and we regularly run a survey about the local coaching market. One question asked is "Who initiated the coaching process?". For years, the results showed an almost equal split: in about one-third of the cases, the client himself initiated the process, in another third of the cases, it was the direct supervisor of the person who participated in the coaching process, and in the rest of the cases, the HR department initiated it. There is also a question about who finances the coaching process: is it paid for from the company budget or as a personal expenditure? At the end of the '90s, many executives felt that participating in a coaching process would be a sign of weakness to the outside world, and these clients paid privately for coaching. Today, coaching is a 'trendy' development tool, and corporate decision-makers allocate a budget for it much more often than they had earlier.

A CEO asked me to coach his direct report, the sales director. In business coaching situations, it is common practice to hold a so-called triangle meeting before beginning the coaching process. In a triangle meeting, the coach sits down with the supervisor who initiated the coaching process for his employee and the future coachee client who will be participating in the process in order to jointly agree on the objective of the process. In the vast majority of these cases, the triangle meeting is about fine-tuning of the objective that has been defined initially: it may be re-worded or slightly changed, but has definitely been confirmed with all parties involved. But this story is different.

The coachee, the sales director, described the current situation and gave an analysis of the problem – the CEO fully agreed. The sales director worked unbelievable hours, about 80(!) hours per week, but still could not make the 10% increase in sales that he and the CEO had set as an objective. He wanted to achieve it in the next six months. When discussing the goals of the coaching process, he also explained that he would like to get support in reducing the hours he worked. At that point, the CEO interrupted: he did not want the sales director to reduce his working hours from 80 to 40 per week, he wanted him to continue working 80 hours, but to more effectively…

This situation proved to me once again how valuable it is to have a triangle meeting to clarify who wants what, and what they are willing to do to reach it.

6

GREEN TEA WITH MILK

Taking small steps as a sure way to progress is a key to any coaching process. This story's coachee wanted to improve his "conflict management skills". His primary goal was to be able to stand up for himself and dare to express his own opinion – even to his supervisor. Apparently he had been struggling all his life with saying "no" or confronting anybody: his subordinates, his secretary or even a waiter at the restaurant. He called this situation "a conflict management" issue.

We met at an elegant café. He ordered a cup of green tea with hot milk. He was served green tea with some cold milk. He was annoyed, but was willing to drink it anyway. Even though this was our very first introductory meeting, I stopped him and asked him if he really wanted to start his self-development process right away.

As the coachee had been avoiding conflict all his life and procrastinating over changes for decades, he instantly said: "Maybe next time." Then he paused briefly and changed his mind.

Coachee: Alright then, let's try to face this conflict. Why don't we ask the waiter to get me another cup of tea?

Coach: I'm sorry, there must be a misunderstanding here. I am not the one who wants to improve my conflict management skills. And I'm not the one who will be confronting the waiter. I am here to confront YOU with how you are behaving – and I just did it.

Coachee: You're right. I think I'll hire you as my coach. Waiter!

This story reminds me of two quotes, one from Helen Keller:

"Avoiding danger is not any safer in the long term than getting a clear perspective. Life is either a great adventure or nothing."[8]

Dan Millman also said, "Peace is not a state without conflicts, it is the state of being able to handle conflicts."[9]

---

8   Helen Keller: *The Open Door*, Doubleday, 1957
9   Dan Millman: *Way of the Peaceful Warrior: A book that changes lives*, Paperback, 2000

CHAPTER 2

The Emperor's New Clothes

EVERYBODY KNOWS ME

In a 2008 presentation, *Charles Handy* cited research data show that over 20 percent of the employees in large corporations never saw their corporate CEO in person. When my coachee claimed that everybody at the company knew him, I became suspicious.

The CEO of a large company was looking for a coach to build up his professional image outside the company. In our first meeting, he talked a lot about himself. It sounded like he was the best CEO in the world: he did everything by the book, everything was going well, and so on. All he wanted to change was to make himself known to the outside world as well. He said he talked to his people a lot, everybody at the company knew him. This sounded unbelievable to me, as there were several thousand employees at the company. I probed him:

"Does everyone really know you at this company?"

"Okay, maybe not every single employee, but all of the people working here at the headquarters."

"Well, then, how do you explain the fact that nobody said 'hello' when we got into the elevator?"

"Oh, it must have just been a coincidence."

"Would you be willing to take a test?"

As it was lunchtime, I suggested that we try the cafeteria. I was surprised when he asked his secretary if he could order à la carte in the cafeteria. On the way from his office to the elevator, it turned out he had never been to the cafeteria during the four years he had been with the company. I suggested that we ride the elevator until somebody said hello to him. The cafeteria remained open until 3 pm, but we would have been left without a meal if we had waited for somebody to greet him.

After this incident, it wasn't difficult to convince him that he first needed to build up an image within his own company, and only afterwards build one outside. As a first step, his photo was posted on the company website, he gave an interview for the corporate newsletter and organized an all-staff meeting – which had never happened before during his four years of service as CEO. Somewhat later, employees started to recognize him in the elevator. He has since become a well-known business person in his community, but it took a long time to get there.

THE POWER OF ECHO

Coachee: I'm looking for a coach for one of my employees. He is often late for deadlines for important tasks and wastes his time with low-priority issues. He really should learn to prioritize.

Coach: I see. Your employee has a different view on priorities than you do, so he misses deadlines.

Coachee: Yes, he has a different view on priorities. But why would he? I am his boss. He should complete the tasks in the order I tell him to.

Coach: I see. Your employee disagrees with you, and even when you tell him in which order you would like him to complete the tasks, he still does not do them that way.

Coachee: He doesn't disagree; he just doesn't do them the way I tell him.

Coach: He doesn't disagree, he just doesn't complete the tasks in the order you tell him to.

Coachee: What do you mean by "in the order I tell him"?

Coach: If I got you right, you have the view that the tasks should be completed in a specific order, and he does not do it that way.

Coachee: Should I tell him in which order he should complete the tasks?

Coach: Well, I thought you had the notion that you, the boss, should tell him the order.

Coachee: I had a notion? Maybe he's not the one who needs a coach?

Coach: If I hear you right, you just put forward another question. Who knows the answer to that one?

Coachee (deep in thought): I got it. He does not need a coach. It's me who needs a coach so that I can tell him clearly what I want him to do: These are the tasks, this is the order of importance and these are the priorities. This will not be easy because he is very stubborn. Perhaps it is better if you coach me, instead of him, because that will help me to improve. Thanks for making me realize this – simply by echoing what I was saying.

9

DOES HE KNOW WHAT YOU EXPECT FROM HIM?

Many coachees look for support in growing from a managerial role to becoming a true leader. I often share with them a quote from *Antoine de Saint Exupery*:

If you want to build a ship, don't drum up the men and women to gather wood, divide the work, and give orders. Instead, teach them to yearn for the vast and endless sea.[10]

This story is about a CEO who was able to give very inspiring speeches about the wonders of the sea, so her team was already building the ship. Still, one day she called me to complain that one of her colleagues was not not completing his tasks the way she would like him to.

Coach: Does he know what you expect from him?

Coachee: I've told him a hundred times how I would like this thing done.

Coach: But did he understand? Does he really know what you expect from him?

Coachee: I just said that I've told him a hundred times.

10 www.brainyquote.com/quotes/quotes/a/antoinedes121261.html

Coach: I'll ask you again, because I didn't get a clear answer: Does he *know* what you expect from him?

Coachee: Aha! Now *I* understand. It's not enough if I just tell him a hundred times; I should check if he really **understood** what I told him. Let's stop this session right now, I'll go back to the office and find out right away. This was our shortest coaching session (lasting 10 minutes), but please send your invoice for the usual one hour because it was at least as valuable as the others. Thank you and I'll see you in two weeks as usual.

This situation reminded me of a quote from *Theodore Roosevelt: The best leader can pick the right men to do what he wants and has enough self-restraint not to interfere with their work.*[11]

11 www.goodreads.com/quotes/147036-the-best-executive-is-the-one-who-has-sense-enough

10

WHAT GETS THE MESSAGE THROUGH

There are coaches who are categorized as 'provocative coaches', I am not one of them. Still, there are times when I have to use provocative means for effect.

Once the owner/CEO of an international company called me with the following problem: his colleagues were not motivated enough, they were not proactive, and lacked the mentality of an owner. At first, he wanted to sign *them* up for coaching – but I told him that this was just passing on responsibility: the boss always has something to do with the motivation of his own people. He disagreed, as he believed motivation must be an inner drive that comes from the individual, not an external one from the supervisor. But he did agree to participate in the coaching process himself.

As a first step, he conducted a Motivation Survey among his people to find out what really motivated them. He did in fact implement some changes: the managers reporting to him were allocated a budget for training and conferences, for networking, and working from home was made an option for one day per week.

In fact, many small steps were made, but after each one, the CEO would merely comment – openly or in private – that he "didn't want to be Santa Claus giving away treats. It's too bad if this is the only way to motivate my people."

As a second step, I had him draw up a list of the distinctive features of *managers and leaders*. But he still did not realize that he was simply a manager himself, not a leader. As he used a lot of quotes from others when speaking, we tried debating using quotes. He quoted Formula 1 racer *Sebastian Vettel: "As soon as money motivates a driver, he cannot be as good as the one with the inner drive."*[12] I used a quote from *basketball star Michael Jordan: "In order to be able to give your best play every day, you must find motivation in everything around you, whatever the message."*[13]

In return, he cited *Kevin McHale: "All the big players motivate themselves."* I quoted *Frank Bettger: "Being able to motivate others is the best-paid skill in the world: firstly because it is so rare, secondly because it is contagious."* From *Anthony Robbins: "People are not lazy. They simply don't have motivating goals."*[14] Finally, from *Dwight David Eisenhower: "Motivation is when*

12 www.theguardian.com/sport/blog/2012/mar/05/sebastian-vettel-red-bull-f1
13 www.brainyquote.com/quotes/authors/m/michael_jordan.html
14 www.brainyquote.com/quotes/quotes/t/tonyrobbin147790.html

you get people to do the things you want, and they think it is what they wanted."[15]

Still nothing. The message hadn't gone through. I was starting to lose my patience, so I said: "So far, we have been beating around the bush. There is a chance that you will fire me as your coach but I'll take the risk and tell you straight away: how do you expect your managers to become leaders – when you are not a leader yourself?"

Then I left. I was quite certain that our coaching process had come to an end. By the time I got home, there was a message in my mailbox: "Now I got it. For weeks, you have been trying to make me realize that the fault lies with me, not my people. You tried your toolbox: a motivational survey, a debate with citations, a list of differences between managers and leaders. The truth is, none of these made me realize what the problem was. What I needed was for you to tell me I was not a leader. Thank you for your honesty. Let's meet again next week, same time, same place."

15 www.brainyquote.com/quotes/quotes/d/dwightdei101562.html

11

A BIRD IS KNOWN BY ITS SONG, A MANAGER BY HIS OFFICE...

You may not realize how much your office reveals about you as a manager. Your employees, customers and suppliers can make presumptions about you based on your office furniture and design. Some managers stuff their office with trophies, memorabilia of former successes. This can be the classic "ego-wall" if they reflect only personal achievements. But if such trophies relate to team effort, they can be motivating for employees.

As a coach, I have seen the offices of many chief executives. I have encountered many interesting things, but people can still surprise me sometimes: such as when I found a gallows standing in an executive's office, given to him as a gift from his subordinates – as related in the following story.

A CEO called a coach to complain that he had a retention problem at his company: he was losing his best people. He wanted to find out the reason, and how he could change the situation. It turned out that his employees did not feel secure in their jobs. There had been major changes to the company structure in the past years: the company had been bought out, then sold again, and directors were moving in and out. The CEO said he didn't understand why his people were still worried, as he had clearly stated at the year-end employee meeting that no more changes were coming up.

As he was explaining this to me, we were sitting in his office. The office had cardboard boxes scattered around, and there were no pictures on the wall: overall it gave the impression of someone who had just moved in. When asked why he had not yet unpacked his things, the CEO explained he was unsure if he was staying in his position. Then he paused to think. He realized there was a gap between what he had just said and what he had been doing so far: he was trying to reassure his own people about job security, but everyone entering his office could see he himself did not feel secure.

There are a lot of small things that can hurt a manager's image. There are personal brand coaches who specialize in this area. But any coach with an eye for such things can suggest that his client remove the teddy bears from his desk or replace a beach party photo of half-naked friends in Bermuda shorts with a copy of his MBA diploma.

Developing one's image as a leader can be especially difficult for those climbing up the career ladder step by step within the same organization. You may end up at the C-level and not realize you are still signing multi-million dollar contracts with a disposable pen – or even worse, one with the competitor's logo printed on it...

12

BUT MY DOOR IS ALWAYS OPEN!

A CFO once called me to discuss how to motivate his employees in times of crisis when he had no budget for bonuses. We ran a motivation survey to find out what would motivate the employees, and got a lot of great ideas. The CFO started to implement them, but there was point he was stuck on: the employee feedback included that they would appreciate it if their boss had an open door policy. The CFO was surprised and frustrated: he had thought that he did in fact keep his office door open.

He brought up the topic at their next staff meeting. His people elaborated on the issue: although the CFO's office door was physically open, when anyone entered to discuss a problem, the CFO kept working on his laptop and hardly looked up, or simply said, 'I'm very busy at the moment. Let's talk about this at another time'.

As a first step to fix the problem, the CFO asked his secretary to put together a list of employees who wanted to see him that day. Then he contacted each of them one by one before the end of the day.

A few weeks later, the CFO asked me to attend one of his staff meetings, observe how he behaved and give him feedback – this is called shadow coaching. At the very beginning of the meeting, he introduced me as his coach, and added that he was using "my support to become an even better manager for you all". I sat through the meeting and, after it was over, I was about to go give my feedback, when one of the staff members stopped me in the hallway:

"I just wanted to have a few words with you so that I could also give you some feedback. I didn't believe in coaching before, but ever since we told him that "open-door" thing was not working, he pays much more attention to us. So I wanted to tell you that you are doing a great job, we can already see the results. But I also want to ask you not to "over-develop" his skills because if he gets promoted to a higher position, we will lose our favorite boss!"

13

HOW LONG IS A WORKDAY?

As a coach, I like to work with clients who understand that being a CEO is not just about driving the best company car and having the top-floor window office but also that, as Ken Blanchard put it: "A leader is a person with authority who is responsible for the result of his subordinates."[16]

There are executives who take their jobs too seriously and end up with a work-life balance problem, like the client in the next story, a newly promoted CEO.

The coaching process was focused on supporting the first 90 days in his new position as CEO so that he would not get drowned in operational issues and automatically follow the patterns of his predecessor, but instead develop his own strategy and make the changes he saw to be necessary. There was no mention of time management or work-life balance.

Once I asked him to participate in a roundtable discussion where executives would be sharing their

16 www.azquotes.com/author/1497-Ken_Blanchard

personal experiences with coaching. During his turn, he made a comment about how relieved he was whenever his wife and son traveled to visit their family out in the countryside – on those nights he could stay late at the office and feel no remorse for missing the nightly bedtime story.

The other roundtable participants, all CEOs, were surprised to hear this: they all left their offices before 6 pm and ate dinners with their families. My client didn't say another word at the event. But during the next coaching meeting, he asked me to change the focus of our coaching process: he would rather turn his CEO position into a "nine-to-five" job.

It is often said that any coach will sooner or later meet a client with an exact same problem that the coach had been personally been faced with earlier. Before becoming a coach, I had worked as a management consultant leading a 140-member project team for a large multinational project. I was 29 then, and many of the team members were twice my age, so I really felt the urge to prove myself. I was often the first to open the office door at 5 am in the morning and would return the key to the security desk late at night. I felt a sense of *déjà vu* with my CEO coaching client.

14

NOBODY CAN CHANGE
PERSONALITIES

A CEO and owner of a medium-sized company called me to help him turn his directors into true leaders. He wanted them to proactively work on strategic issues and not just sit around and wait for him to come up with a vision. I listened carefully and agreed that a director should be not only a good manager, but a true leader as well.

What about the CEO, though? Surely he had made tons of mistakes before while turning into a leader himself. And surely he was still now making some mistakes in his attempt to turn his directors into true leaders. Micro-management is one typical such mistake: a CEO who oversee all operational matters himself or approves every single bank transfer clearly demonstrates a lack of trust in his people. With such a role model at the top, how could any director become a true leader?

I read in a coaching book once that some clients prefer to work with coaches in such a way where they act as if they were slaves, with the coach as the slave-driver, and thus hand all responsibility for the outcome of the coaching process over to the coach. I was astonished when I read this, as all my previous clients had been very active and equal participants in the coaching process. But now this CEO was telling me,

"Laura, I would like you to take the lead in this coaching process. I will do whatever you tell me, but you are in charge of driving the whole process."[17]

I reflected what he had just said right back at him: he would willingly give up his leadership position in the coaching process, while at the same time claiming that he is a true role model for leadership for his employees. I suggested that he should read Howard Shultz's *Pour Your Heart Into It: How Starbucks Built a Company One Cup at a Time*. He did and he continued the coaching process as if he had been reborn a different man.

---

17 Howard Schultz: *Pour your heart into it: How Starbucks built a company one cup at a time,* Paperback 1999

15

SHADOW COACHING

Shadow coaching is a special session during which the coach follows the coachee like a shadow. They may attend a presentation or a meeting together, but each time the coach is only briefly introduced with the words, "This is my coach, here to help me become a better leader". The coach only observes, does not interfere, and gives face-to-face feedback to the coachee at the end of the session. The goal is not to play "Big Brother" by reporting that "the young guy in the checkered shirt was playing Minecraft the whole time you were talking", but is more about letting the manager know that there might have been people who were "untouched" by his words.

One time, a male manager was completely oblivious to the fact that a woman was forced to stand throughout an entire meeting while all her male colleagues were sitting – there was no seat left for her. In Hungary, this is a very major breach of etiquette. It should not be a surprise that this company was not very popular among women, and it was hard to reach the goal of increasing the proportion of female managers as an important KPI defined by the global headquarters.

On another occasion, I was coaching the vice president of a large company that was also registered on the stock market. He needed a coach for reflection, because he had the feeling that he was getting less and less objective feedback every time he was promoted to a higher position. He had very few encounters with the global vice president (his immediate boss), but he always received a positive performance appraisal from him – so he didn't really know whether he needed to improve, or how. It seemed a bit awkward, but he wanted to pay somebody to tell him about his weaknesses in business life – since his wife ensured that he heard about his personal weaknesses every day.

So we began with a Marshall Goldsmith test listing 21 behaviors that could help you in the beginning of your career, but which could later became barriers to success in a top management position. He asked his colleagues to complete an online survey to serve as a good baseline for further measures. He received some feedback that he didn't really understand and wanted to investigate further.

He asked me to attend a board meeting as his shadow and then provide some very honest feedback. I was quite surprised by the fact that the invitation did not contain the agenda, even though the planned duration of the meeting was four hours. It was hard for me to imagine how effective it could be sitting together for four hours, but I tried to keep an open mind about the situation. Five minutes into the meeting I might as well have left the room because the meeting took on a pattern that remained unchanged until the end of the discussion and which was quite typical for his management style. The vice president entered the room and said, "It's hot in here." Five of the board members immediately jumped up from their seats to open up windows. Luckily, only one could be opened, and only partially.

CHAPTER 3

The Little Match Girl

16

GLOBAL COMPANY, LOCAL CHALLENGES

The release of my first English-language book took place in the PWC Centre in London. The HR director of a global company also attended the event, and we had a chat afterwards.

The company operates in 160 countries, and there had been a strict tradition of always selecting country managers from current employees who had already climbed the corporate ladder. A few years previously, however, they had decided to change this process and recruited ten of the 160 country managers from outside the company. Some of them relocated to their new jobs from other countries, some had worked in different industries, but all of them had taken various different paths during their careers. In each case, the selection process took almost a year, because the company wanted to make a very well-considered choice. The applicants had to fill out evaluation tests, attend personal interviews at the company's American headquarters, go through a three-day assessment center, and work for a week on a presentation about what they would do for the company if they were selected. All this shows that the selection process was a very elaborate one. However, only two of the ten externally recruited country managers were still with the company by the end of that year; the rest of them had quit their jobs.

At that time, the idea of restoring the previous selection process was again considered, but they also wanted to give successfully changing the company culture another chance. The selection process still remained long and elaborate, but they wanted to find a solution that would ease the isolation and loneliness of the newcomers – as this was a problem that was uncovered during the exit interviews. All of the remaining new recruits were assigned an internal mentor, one of the other 150 country managers within the company, as well as an external coach.

The HR director told me that they were seeking coaches and that I had a chance to be a part of the process. Remembering the things I have learned about questions, I thanked him for the opportunity and asked for some time to come back with an answer. Arriving home, I told my husband about the opportunity. He was very excited about it and told me that I should take on the challenge, since there was really nothing to lose, and we didn't have to tell anyone; meaning that no one would know whether or not I was selected to be one of the ten coaches. Suffering from stomach cramps and knowing the fact that being a Hungarian woman raised in a formerly communist country meant that my English would never be the same as that of an English or American coach, I gave it a shot. I talked to each of the ten new recruits on the phone to introduce myself and get to know their problems.

To my great surprise, six out of the ten candidates chose me to be their coach. I was very anxious before each session, but I tried to relax by telling myself that they were the ones who chose me, not the other way around. I learned a lot about myself and about managing intercultural challenges during that year.

The project turned out to be a great success: the ratio of people wanting to leave the company decreased substantially, eight out of the ten newly appointed directors wanted to stay on. (I was personally very sorry about the fact that the two who left were the two women.) Our joint efforts were successful: the mentor-coach support proved to be helping the new people settle into their new roles.

The coachees were all very different people with very different backgrounds. There was a South Korean, a Brazilian, a Dutch person, a Briton, an American and one from an Arab country, so one could really say that a full range of intercultural diversity was being covered. Not only did I never see my Arab coachee face-to-face, I had to remove my photo from my CV, and we were not allowed to use Skype; we could only converse via a secured landline. During one of the sessions, he told me that he had appeared on CNN and wanted to send me the link to the interview to get my feedback on it. I was anxious to click on the link and watch the video, which turned out to feature two men with similar-sounding voices, one wearing a suit and the other in traditional Arab dress. Even today, I still do not know which one I was coaching.

Since their common goal was to feel good about themselves in their new position and fit well into the company, we took time right from the beginning to talk about things that they felt were stressful. One of them quickly claimed that he never experienced any work-related stress and did not feel the need to talk about it. He could sense my surprise, so he briefly explained that this had absolutely nothing to do with me. A few years earlier he had been sailing in the Pacific Ocean when he was attacked by pirates. For two days, he found himself floating in the ocean hanging onto a ten-square-foot wooden board. Since this experience – as far as he was concerned – the term "work-related stress" had ceased to exist. I thanked him for the explanation and asked him no more questions about stress.

With a definite purpose in mind, we focused on things that had gone well, things that they were happy about, successful at and proud of. One of my coachees had previously been a vice president at the World Bank. He told me that, for him, the joy of life meant being free, and not having to fly every day to work by helicopter and not being surrounded by bodyguards. The little joys of everyday life…

17

DO TRY IT AT HOME
– THE BENEFIT
OF POSITIVE GOSSIP

I was coaching the managing director of an IT company, who one day came to one of our sessions with the following topic: December is always very hectic at the company, there is a lot of overtime and an increased number of conflicts, with everybody growing very tense. It would be so nice to have better cooperation between the team members just before the holidays, in the spirit of kindness, instead of dwelling on other people's weaknesses. Moreover, how nice it would be for the people to realize that if the entire staff shows up for work, no one will have to do anyone else's jobs.

So he gave me some insight (including many details) into the current situation and also described the "desired" future state. Then we began to collect alternative ideas on how the goal could be achieved. Since the staff was made up of IT specialists, and many of them were very introverted, his first idea was to come up with an online questionnaire that everybody could fill out and provide some feedback while sitting comfortably at their own computers. So for the next session, his homework was to complete a Johari window exercise with his team.

The outcome was very positive: all the people were very happy to receive a list about all those of their positive personal qualities they were already aware of, and also to find that others were aware of them too. It was also pleasant to learn that there were some qualities they had missed in their self-assessment, but which some of the others found noteworthy. So at the next session, he explained that some of the staff members were using this Johari window[18] as their screen saver, while others had printed it out and displayed it by their desk. He had also overheard some people saying that all this activity had become a lively topic of conversation and the employees had started talking to each other in a more positive way.

However, the manager still thought that there was something missing from the feedback. He said that the Johari window was a great technique, but it limits the number of qualities to 50 choices, and he wanted to see another tool that makes it possible to give feedback on specific experiences or actions that generated positive emotions in others. He also suggested that, after seeing the positive results from the first round, maybe the staff now would be brave enough to get up from their monitors and come out of their "shells". But no sooner had he started talking about how nice it would be for everyone to sit in a circle and hear about their good deeds from their colleagues, then he vetoed himself

18 For a Johari window please see: businesscoach.hu/en/johari

and said that this would be a very uncomfortable thing to do, even for himself, and he'd rather not try it after all. He said it would be nice to hear what good things the others had to say about him, but definitely not with his face visible to the others, should he blush or show an emotional reaction, heaven forbid. But maybe he could sit with his back turned to the circle.

Well, this is exactly how positive gossip works. As he talked about it, he fell in love with his very own idea, but at the same time he was unsure about whether this could be done in his team. He asked me whether I had ever experienced anything like this before and what the outcome was. I told him that I had done a similar activity several times, and every time it had turned out very well, but I absolutely understood his concerns nonetheless. He decided that he would rather not take this on as his homework assignment, but he promised to think about the idea.

In the end, he decided that he liked the idea so much, he tried it out on Saint Nicholas Day with his family: his wife, their four kids and the four grandparents. It turned out so well that he didn't even wait until the next coaching session to try it out with his team as well. Although it was a coaching process focused on business and work-oriented goals, it had positive effects on the family as well – and it has since become part of their Saint Nicholas Day tradition.

18

AHA MOMENTS WITH LEGO

Whenever we run coach training, I always emphasize that an experienced coach can turn anything into a coaching tool, and I encourage the participants not to restrict themselves to the 150 tools we introduce in our methodology handbook[19] but to be bold and rely on their own creativity. I am pleased to see when coach training courses, as they often do, end with an exam where students, sometimes working in pairs, present their own independently created coaching tool. Almost all well-known toys have appeared so far in the exams, including colorful beads, the "Who is Who" board game, pebbles, roulette chips and of course, the ever-fascinating LEGO products.

Once I was coaching the director of a large tele-communications company. I think it will say a lot about his personality if I mention that I have always used the informal form of address with all of my clients – except for him. His office was decorated solely with posters of the products made by his company. No signs of his personal life at all. Everything was perfectly arranged, as orderly as the inside of a nuclear reactor. We made

19 Laura Komocsin: *Toolful Coach: SPARKLE coaching model with 150 useful tools and case studies*, Amazon, 2012

good progress with the coaching sessions, and he mentioned being satisfied several times, so I felt that a certain amount of trust had developed between us. But he was not an easy-going type of person, so it was risky to choose any type of toy or game for his coaching process. Chances were good that I might easily destroy the trust we had built. One day he brought up a subject that made my instincts tell me: get the LEGO figures out on the table!

I gave him my usual introductory sentences about how this coaching process was all about him, about his goals, and that if he felt that we were going in the wrong direction, then he should let me know immediately. He nodded anxiously. At that point I took 50 LEGO figures out of my bag. The air froze. It was that classic coaching silence when we know better than to say anything. I waited. He looked at me, then at the LEGO figures. Back and forth. Then he spoke:

"Laura, I am truly surprised. I had thought of you as a serious person. That is the reason why I selected you instead of the many other coaches. I am a very serious person. I am a person who is well respected in public. My colleagues look up to me. Everything we have done in the coaching sessions so far has been to my advantage. So I am willing to give this a chance as well. But please do not take this as an offense: I want to have the door locked. I really wouldn't want my secretary to catch us playing LEGO during an expensive business coaching session."

I reassured him that I did not take it as an offense. He locked the door.

And then he had an AHA moment. After carefully selecting and arranging the LEGO figures that most resembled his team members, he spoke:

"Oh, now I see why this manager who reports to me is so incapable! All of his colleagues have a weapon, but he does not! He doesn't even have a shield to protect himself with."

Shortly afterwards, he had another AHA moment.

"It is so obvious that we can win this game! We have a bigger team and there are only droids on the other side. I will take this challenge!"

A few sessions later, when my gut feeling signaled that it was time to play LEGO again, he no longer felt any need to lock the door. What's more, during our final session, he even asked me to please call him by his first name.

19

INTROVERTED OR EXTROVERTED COACHEES

We coach many successful introverted managers whose strength is being a good listener. This means that their chances of becoming a leader are much better when a coaching approach is taken. Nevertheless, it is essential for them to become "visible" in the organization and consciously work on being more extroverted in order to achieve their career goals. One of my coachees with such a mentality once confessed to me that as a child she had wanted to become a librarian. But, to her parents' prompting, she went for a business degree and started to climb the career ladder at a multinational company. Although it required immense effort, she succeed in her job. However, when I asked her about her dreams, she'd say that is having the White Knight come and save her – while she is working in a children's library. While her dream is being realized, she'll develop her leadership skills with her coach and climb further on the career ladder.

I also know of another case that fits this storyline. A coach asked the coachee to rate how introverted she thought she was on a scale of one to ten, with one being extremely introverted and ten being extremely extroverted. Her reply was "zero". The next logical question was to find out how much she wanted to change. The answer she gave was "two", and this was set as the goal. This meant that the distance between the starting point of the process and the goal was quite far. The woman worked in the pharmaceutical industry, managing a team of 80 people, who all shared a large open-space office. The employees started work at 8 am, but she would only arrive around 8:30, because she took her kids to school in the morning. So when she arrived at the office each morning, the others were already working. She thought it was better not to say "hello" to anyone, in order not to disturb them in their work. Of course, several people took this for rudeness. She spoke flawless French and English, but every time she attended a business dinner in Brussels or Paris, she would spend half the time in the restroom, dreading having to come back to the table. As soon as she did return, she would start eating right away in order to avoid having to get involved in the conversation around her, since her mouth was full…

The coaching process did not result in her becoming fully extroverted, but she did attain the defined level of "two", and felt she had even reached as far as 2.75. At the end of the coaching process, she said, "Before we started the coaching process, I was thinking about getting a folding screen to have a barrier around my desk in the office. Since my boss did not consent to this, I thought maybe I could get a really large monitor to hide behind. As I don't need the folding screen any longer, I saved a lot of money for my company, so we could actually say that the coaching was for free."

Another one of my clients was the manager of the IT Department in a bank. Thinking of typical stereotypes, I was expecting to meet a stiff and introverted person, but to my surprise he was quite the opposite. Following a short introduction, he started explaining the reason why he wanted a coach. He was successful at his job; however, he had a bad habit of fooling around and playing practical jokes. As a result, his peers had lost respect for him. Up to a certain point, the VP had always protected him whenever he got up to his tricks. For example, he just smiled when they organized a competition of rolling office chairs through the lobby or threw paper airplanes out of the 15th floor window aiming to hit a small puddle in the street. But one time he just pushed it too far. Since he was responsible for the IT system, he came up with the idea of tricking his colleagues with their own computers. When they signed in to their computers the next morning, the logo and welcome screen of a competing bank appeared – the one that was rumored to be about to buy out their current employer. He found this to be very funny, but his boss had a different opinion: he was furious!

In our coaching sessions, we assessed his current situation, and he prepared a SWOT analysis of himself. He said that he had always considered his sense of humor to be a strength, one which – in his opinion – the bank could further exploit; however the opinion of his boss was exactly the opposite. My coachee was sure that he wanted to stay with his employer, he respected his boss and liked his colleagues, but he did not want to suppress this quality in himself, because he felt it was valuable. We discussed previous occasions when he had used his sense of humor with no harm being caused, as well as cases which ended up in a conflict. As he analyzed these situations, he found a pattern, and was able to define topics that were "OK" to make fun of and those colleagues who were "safe to joke around with". He compiled a nice, shiny matrix and asked his boss to approve it – after solemnly promising that he would never again make a joke of a competing bank involved in buyout rumors. Instead, he'd take part in organizing an April Fool's Day event and participate proactively in the semi-annual team building events; moreover, he'd be more than happy to lend his "entertainment skills" to other departments in the company. Some departments were happy to collaborate with him – for example Marketing and Public Relations, and even Human Resources involved him in a brand new social media recruiting process. He added these new associates in fun to his matrix, as well as safe and unsafe topics to handle with them. This allowed him to further support his bank in its business success. Whenever he was unsure about whether a given situation was suitable for a joke, he could always go back to the matrix, or in case of doubt he could get approval from his boss.

20

NEVER TOO LATE TO PRAISE

The CEO of an IT company called me as a coach to help him with the high turnover problem he had. Based on the exit interview records, departing employees complained that they had been kept busy as workers, but felt their work was not appreciated. They never received a "thank you" or a "well done". The CEO offered two comments on this fact:

1. "If there had been any problems with them, I would have told them."
2. "Couldn't they see I'm satisfied when I gave them a bonus or a pay raise?"

The CEO took it for granted that his employees would deliver good quality and therefore made no comments on it. If there was a delay or mistake, he always promptly pointed this out. But he had no vocabulary for appraisal or appreciation, and so his people were losing motivation and were reluctant to come up with new creative ideas in fear of making mistakes.

I pushed the CEO to identify those situations where he could have offered positive feedback, but had not. It turned out that the coachee's behavior was not limited only to his company, he also operated the same way in his private life: he took high-level performance for granted when it came to his kids and wife at home too.

When faced with these observations, he decided he wanted to change this attitude of his so that he would not lose any more of his best people. But in order to develop the new habit of giving positive feedback, he needed to start with small steps.

As a first task, he was asked to praise his three-year-old daughter for learning to use the playground swing alone. Now he could read his magazines when he took her out to play, and did not have to push her any more. He came to the next coaching session proudly saying that it was such a good feeling for his daughter to get positive feedback from her dad, and it was also a very good feeling for him.

He was so satisfied with this development that he decided to praise his wife for something she did right. But when our next coaching session came around, he arrived frustrated. He said he had not done his homework because his wife had not done anything that would have been worth praising. I was a bit skeptical, so I asked him to tell me what kind of family activities they had engaged in over the past few weeks. He mentioned that his younger son had been baptized the Sunday before.

"Now I am really impressed: you are managing a market-leading IT company and yet you still had time to organize the family lunch, to invite all the relatives, to buy all the presents and the suit for your son! You would be a real catch for any woman!" I was being sarcastic, but this was what finally got the message through. Although this session ended up lasting longer than usual, he found at least three things he could appreciate and thank his wife for.

As for his people at the office, he picked the one who deserved appreciation the most. Then the one whom he most wanted to make sure he would retain. And he also picked the employee who would be least astonished to finally receive positive feedback: the CEO was afraid he would be laughed at if his employees discovered he was taking classes from a coach in giving positive feedback.

Finally, results started to show. Although not solely a result of the coaching, employee turnover dropped from 20% to 7%. And other stakeholders also benefited: the CEO's wife called me before Christmas to thank me. She had been against coaching earlier, as it would take away even more of the CEO's precious time from his family, but she eventually discovered it was doing a great deal to improve their personal lives as well. And now she is expecting their third child.

CHAPTER 4

The Snow Queen

21

I´M NOT YOUR FRIEND, BUDDY!

I was on my way to introduce myself to the CEO of a company with two thousand employees. They had called me because it was hard for the CEO to "mind his manners". He was not able to judge when to be formal or informal, and to judge how far he could go with his jokes. He regularly succeeded in making top managers (and not only female ones) burst into tears, and once sparked a political scandal at a press conference, where he completely deprived a journalist of his dignity.

A specific short story perfectly illustrates his character: There was a huge event marking the opening of a factory, with thousands of people attending. The CEO said into the microphone that he had asked the prime minister to come and cut the ribbon with the national colors. Then he continued: "Our prime minister is not very quick, but I can understand: why hurry if there will be an election next month?"

He was not afraid of anybody.

I took a deep breath before entering his office. As I did, I saw he was looking in the opposite direction, showing his back to me. I greeted him loudly.

– Hi John! I believe I am only a few years younger than you, so you won't mind if I call you by your first name!

He turned around, already fuming with anger.

– Good afternoon! I believe we have never met, and I am the CEO of a huge company and I am at least ten years older than you. I am not your pal! I'm not your friend, buddy! How do you dare to call me by my first name?

– How does it feel?

– What do you mean how does it feel?

He was about to burst with rage.

– How does it feel that I did not follow the rules of courtesy?

– What you do mean how does it feel? I'm going to explode in a moment! How do you dare? Who are you? God Almighty? I once had an American star coach, but even he didn't dare to take it this far!

– I'm sorry, but do you remember why you were seeking a coach?

– Oh, you mean this was a game? Well, I felt awful. You are terrible! We haven't even come to terms yet, and you have already taken a very risky chance – for free? Wow, I'm amazed! Now you can call me by my first name.

22

GENERAL, SIR!

Many years ago, a company was looking for a coach for its deputy CEO. He wanted to move on with his career at its international headquarters in a different country within the next year. In the meantime he was planning to train his future successor, who was at that time not yet ready to take over his duties.

"I am not a good person. My colleagues call me by my last name, the same way I call them, or they just call me the "General". I make decisions very quickly and autocratically. I don't care about other peoples' opinions because I know my business well and I know how to make good decisions. I am the manager, I don't see the need to involve others in the decision-making process."

I am not a life coach, but I believe that if an executive does something well in the workplace, then he should implement the beneficial practice in his private life as well – and vice versa. For this reason, although I never intentionally dig deep into the private life of the coachee, I do to the point where this aspect becomes transparent. So I asked the coachee how he made decisions in his private life. He told me how – but something just didn't feel right about it. I became suspicious and I thought I would ask him why he chose me to be his coach.

"My wife saw you on a TV show and she told me that you were the best," he said. It turned out that his wife made most of the decisions at home.

The coachee used the phrase "as a man would say" suspiciously often. I happened to have a deck of 200 personal qualities cards (100 positive and 100 negative) in my bag. So I asked him to divide the cards into two piles: which of them were the feminine qualities and which were masculine?

He did so and finally summarized what he thought: "To make decisions in an autocratic way, without consulting others: this is masculine. To speak loudly, to curse: this is also masculine because women do not talk like this. I understand that I should be more empathic to be a CEO, but do not 'overcoach' me, because I may become impotent in the end!"

I had coached a lot of women who had problems with their feminine sides, and I referred this man to a psychologist as well.

23

A DYSLEXIC MANAGER

A manager called me once to explain that he was having difficulties controlling his emotions at the workplace, and often yelled at his people. We used the SPARKLE coaching model to gain an understanding of his Situation, define his goal for Positioning and came to the Alternatives phase, where we started to collect ideas on how to reach his goal. He was very engaged and creative in brainstorming what he could do and what resources he could use. Again and again, he commented that it would be most efficient for him in terms of time and energy for him if he could use communicate orally instead of in writing. After some time, I decided to confront him with this in a direct way: I told him he was acting as if he was afraid of something. "Why don't you want to send that out in writing? Can't you write an email?" I asked without thinking.

There was a long silence. I felt I had stumbled upon something painful. It turned out that the manager was dyslexic and that is why he avoided written communication. He always presented without notes and he used the phone instead of email.

The next week, I took my baby daughter to a physiologist. The specialist explained how important it was for my daughter to crawl properly because many children who skip this phase of development end up with some kind of learning disorder like dyslexia. She also explained that she had had adult patients whom she needed to teach how to crawl so that their disability could be helped. In fact, results showed up within weeks.

This piece of information was really helpful with my coaching client. I felt horrible that I might have hurt him with my question and I really wanted to make up for my mistake. All turned out well in the end: my client went to visit the physiotherapist I recommended, and finally started to use more written communication and was able to better control his emotions.

As a coach, you should know your limitations and not be afraid of referring your clients to specialists if doing so would better serve their needs.

24

HOLD UP A TIE, RATHER THAN YELL

A CEO hired me to help him with his anger-control issues: he would often get upset and start yelling at his people. He was asked to keep a record of how often this happened over a two-week period, also noting why the yelling started and who was involved. It turned out the problem was primarily work-related and it only occurred at his office. Most often, it was his directors he yelled at, in their management meetings.

To provide some background on his career, he explained that he had started working for this company right out of college. He had climbed the corporate ladder up to the very top. He went a long way back with his directors, and had known many of them since their student years together, and their families also kept in close contact, traveling together for holidays and so on. The CEO recognized that he started yelling when he had a conflict with one of these directors who was also an old buddy: management meetings were often very informal and may have looked democratic – but when it came time to make a decision, the CEO had the final say and he often yelled it out loud in order to demonstrate he was the boss. He always felt bad about it afterwards and would apologize repeatedly. He really wanted to change this pattern. He thought if he could get a few moments to calm down, then he could regain his self-control and avoid yelling.

He felt he was not able to keep quiet and count to three inside: he needed to do something right at that moment. We brainstormed ideas for what he could do: smash the table, which was not very professional, or else come up with a standard sentence like:

"Now I should count to three in order to spare you the yelling." At the next management meeting, he tried this. It was somewhat better, but still not working the way he had wanted it to. He decided he would combine the sentence with some kind of movement. First he came up with this: he would take his glasses off and raise his palm over his eyes. When he first tried this, his directors thought he had grown suddenly ill. So this didn't work, either. Then he tried rolling up his sleeves. He got laughed at. Then he had another idea.

The previous CEO had been a very strict and uptight man. He never made friends with anybody, and always wore a tie: all day and all week. When he retired, he received a gift box of seven ties (one for every day – including the weekend as well) as a farewell present.

All the directors remembered him and his ties very well. He had left the current CEO one of his ties as a keepsake.

So the next time when the current CEO was getting upset in a management meeting, he recited his standard "count-until-three" sentence and walked over to his desk to show off the tie he had inherited. Everybody recognized it and got the message. The CEO did not have to yell any longer and still was taken seriously. By a few months later, the inherited tie was no longer required, and the yelling stopped completely.

25

ASK ANYTHING,
EXCEPT ON-CALL DUTY

One time I was called by the European director of a global pharmaceutical company to coach one of their country managers. The country manager had been working for the company for many years, they were satisfied with his work, but lately they had noticed that he was "getting tired". Therefore they decided to offer him assistance in finding the right balance between work and private life. There is another risk inherent in a case like this, because the manager could end up suffering from burnout or – even worse – taking a long sabbatical or quitting his job altogether.

After receiving the necessary input from the client's HR representative, I was asked to meet the coachee and inform the HR representative if anything else could be done to assist the coaching process. The company really wanted to retain this employee.

So I met with the country manager. I listened to the story from his point of view, talked about his team and the kind of work he did, things he did not have time for, reasons for taking a sabbatical, or even changing jobs. He set his goal for the near future: to make time to go to work out once a week and to spend more quality time with his family in the evenings – meaning to go home earlier and not to continue working at home. Next, we assessed the possible ways for him to achieve his goal. We identified the tasks he should reject, the ones he should delegate, and others where he needed more resources: this "wish list" was then ready to be handed over to his boss.

During our second telephone conversation my coachee's boss reiterated how important it was for the company to keep this colleague and to reinstate his work-life balance. Fantastic, I thought: with such strong support, we were destined to succeed. So I started to discuss the coachee's "wish list" with his boss.

– The country manager wants to insource a recently outsourced task because the quality of work has become much worse since the outsourcing. It requires extra time for him to monitor and implement corrections.

– Alright. It seemed like a good idea to outsource this activity, but since it has not worked out – let's go back to the previous model.

– He wants to hire 40 people to work for the second largest business unit.

– Okay. If he believes this would help to restore his work-life balance, let's do so.

– He wants to have a budget of X thousand euros to spend on a Business Process Reengineering Project in another business area.

– Alright.

– He has 79 days of unused vacation time. He has been rolling over these days for years, so he wants to take them out as follows: one long weekend every month and two weeks of vacation every quarter.

– Alright.

– In order to have a really peaceful vacation, he wants to recruit a reliable, very experienced top manager from another firm to join the company and become his deputy.

– Alright.

– He would like to ask you not to schedule regular conference calls after 5 pm.

I could hear the person take a deep breath at the other end of the line, and his vehemence was suddenly forming into words as he talked:

– What the hell is he thinking? This is a global company with ongoing production in every possible time zone of this planet. Any executive like him – with such a large company car and a benefit package – is not supposed to whine about such things, but instead be available 24 hours a day!

At this point I had to give him some feedback, stating that I heard him raising his voice and that I suppose this latter wish had made him very angry. Suddenly, he started to complain.

– I have been working for this company forever. I work 24/7 at all times. My marriage has collapsed, I've lost connection with my kids and my colleagues. I don't even understand the term "work-life balance", since work always comes first. And there is work all the time.

Again, I had to give him feedback. I told him that his active support so far had made me believe very strongly in the success of this coaching process. Now that it had turned out he could not serve as a role model in the process, it would be very hard to accomplish any kind of results with the country manager.

At that point he realized he needed a coach as well.

26

ACTING AS A ROLE MODEL
AT A TEAM BUILDING EVENT

Coaches sometimes have the opportunity to observe their clients in both their usual work environment and in uncommon situations. Shadow coaching – following the client as a shadow throughout an entire working day or just one event – is the tool used by coaches to gather first-hand experience about how the coachee behaves in various situations. Such an event can be an important presentation, a regular team meeting, or it can be an outdoor team building event like in the story below.

One time a manager was complaining to me, as his coach, that his people were not straightforward with him: they were cooking the numbers, and he couldn't see the real picture. He expected his employees to be honest with him and to have enough courage to share bad news, even at the risk of making him angry. His clear expectation was frank and open communication. I asked the client what he thought about role models. The client explained he did believe in the importance of positive role models for others, and he considered himself to be a role model for his people.

During the coaching process I had the opportunity to shadow the manager during a team building event with his people. It was an outdoor event in the woods. For a start, each team member was dropped at a different place in the forest and had to find his own way to the base. It was getting dark, and they had no help at hand: no maps, no mobile phones, nothing. However, the manager used a GPS tracker – although this was clearly against the rules…

In the evening, the guys went to the gym to release the stress. They competed in doing push-ups. The manager cheated this time as well: he started later than the others…

As a final twist, it turned out the manager was also cheating on his wife. He used the entry card of a subordinate to leave the building so that his absences could not be traced to his own card.

After the team-building event, I repeated to him what he had said earlier: "Acting as a role model is really important!" He nodded.

"Does this mean that you cannot expect your team to be honest?"

He agreed. Then I reminded him about the three occasions when he had cheated, and I asked whether he wanted to change himself or just his team. He thought about this for a while, and thanked me for holding up the mirror to see his own reflection.

As a farewell, he promised to call me the next day to schedule the next coaching session.

He never called me again.

CHAPTER 5

The Princess and the Pea

GETTING FIRED OR SHARING KNOWLEDGE?

When an airplane crashes, the cause of the accident can usually not be attributed to one single factor, but rather to a chain of events involving at least six or seven failures or mistakes. If there were only a single error, this could be easily eliminated by control measures – but in most of the cases, one error triggers a chain reaction. If dirt gets into the system, and then neither the pilot nor the co-pilot is sufficiently cautious, and then this is compounded by a mistake in the control tower, and so on. For a tragedy to happen, multiple causes are required. After the incident, all the causes are carefully examined, and, wherever possible, the process is improved. Similarly to the aviation industry, extraordinary care is required in the case of nuclear power plants and in the pharmaceutical industry. Although this may seem less obvious, an IT firm can also experience incidents that result in serious consequences.

One of my clients arrived at our coaching session in a very bad mood. He had been forced to fire one of his colleagues that day. Our topic for the session was to discuss what happened, what went well, what he learned from the situation and what the things he should do differently in the future. His colleague had made a number of mistakes in his job, resulting in the crash of the entire ATM network all over the country for several hours. This was not only a nuisance for bank customers – they could not withdraw money until several hours later – but it also resulted in a serious financial loss for the bank and damaged its image. The manager had felt that he needed to make an example of the case by firing the employee at fault. He had gone ahead and done so, but nevertheless he felt very bad about it, because deep in his heart he was unsure whether he had done the right thing. His uncertainty was partially due to his personal engagement with the situation – considering the many years they had spent together as colleagues through thick and thin – and also the fact that the colleague was the father of five children. Moreover, he was a very talented professional, which meant that the company had also lost a valuable expert.

My client wanted to leave our session with an action plan to ease his bad conscience and also a plan for how to help his former colleague find a new job. His other goal was to create an action plan in case of a similar situation happened in the future, and one to handle it without losing valuable human resources and knowledge. I asked him to give me both a detailed description of the factors that would satisfy him and a description of the new process. As he spoke, his plan was beginning to take shape around the following solution: if something similar should happen again, he would not immediately fire the employee but instead would give him a choice: he could take either the official sanction (immediate termination or a documented warning, depending on the seriousness of the mistake) or publicly take the blame. In this latter case, he would have to take responsibility for his mistake, take part in the corrective measures, and prepare a presentation about the lessons learned, which he would then present in a "road show" to talk to other colleagues about the event in order to help avoid similar mistakes in the future.

Unfortunately for the company and my client, they did not have to wait long for the next incident to occur. Only a few weeks after the ATMs crashed, there was a similar failure, and my client had a chance to test his new protocol. In a neighboring country, all mobile devices used by government employees stopped working for half a day. Politicians are loud and have a lot of influence – regardless of their country of origin. My client had to take immediate action. The situation was rescued as quickly as possible, and within the company, the problem and the solution were made public in an internal road show.

Regarding the two stories above, my client also explained that previously there had been no real knowledge-sharing within their company, and mistakes were unacceptable, which meant that people were afraid of being punished. This kind of company culture was a real barrier to learning from mistakes – either from your own or from somebody else's. My client knew they could not change the company culture within a day or two. But he also knew that being a top manager gave him a good opportunity to shape that culture step by step. It was around this time that Carol Dweck published her book *Growth Mindset*[20] and was being featured at an author event in Budapest. I called my coachee to invite him to join me for the event, in order to get some inspiration. He accepted. So the change started, and more and more people decided to go along with it.

20 Carol Dweck: *Mindset: The New Psychology of Success,* Ballantine Books New York, 2007

28

BECOMING TOO ASSERTIVE

Do not overuse your strengths! This was the motto of a workshop organized by Harvard Business Review, where participants shared stories on how a personal strength can be developed and exploited – or over-developed and over-exploited. One story was about an executive who had previously been overly pessimistic, then started to change thanks to the feedback he received. But in the end, he became too optimistic and too bold in taking risks – and the company almost went bankrupt. Another manager wanted to change his authoritative management style and ended up with a democratic decision-making process that required weeks, so it slowed down the company procedures so much that they almost lost their competitiveness.

A CEO called me to support one of his managers in becoming more assertive in dealing with their suppliers. The manager preferred to avoid conflicts and thus was not very effective in protecting the company's interests against suppliers. He could not enforce tighter deadlines or better quality, and when it came to a non-fulfillment of delivery, the CEO had to step in to reprimand the supplier.

The manager himself wanted to change and become more assertive, as he also suffered from not being able to stand up for himself. With coaching support, he stepped out of his comfort zone and asserted himself in increasingly important issues. One day the CEO asked me to see him in his office and said:

"I am very pleased that our company interests are now being well represented with the suppliers. You have done a good job of increasing my manager's assertiveness. Maybe too good of a job, in fact. I've realized he is being more assertive with me as well. I would like you to stop coaching him and start working with me now, so that I can also assert myself when talking to him."

29

NOTHING IS GOOD ENOUGH

A financial director was complaining that his staff was not proactive enough. He thought he needed to soften his leadership image so that his employees would not be afraid to share their ideas with him. He worked with me as his coach for weeks, making progress in small steps. Once he reported that earlier that week his team had come up with a bunch of new ideas for changes in their business area. I felt really proud of my work and thought that the process had come to a happy ending. But the director did not share my feelings.

Although he liked some of the ideas his staff had collected, and he appreciated their proactivity, he was still not pleased. He disliked the way the ideas were presented: "They really could have spent some time turning these into a proper presentation format, not just a few sheets of notepad paper," he commented bitterly. Nothing was good enough for him, in fact.

A similar story from the non-corporate world: the husband of a friend of mine was a passionate poker player and was participating in a major competition.

He thought that he would be happy to finish the tournament among the top ten – out of thousands of players.

He returned home, early in the morning, after a long night of poker and woke his wife fully disappointed: in the end he had come in second, but within an inch of winning...

Finally the truth struck me: these two people were one and the same man, behaving similarly in both his private and his professional lives, so when he started to work on it, the change had very positive effects on both of these areas of his lives.

30

COMPATIBILITY ISSUE

The owner and CEO of an IT company asked me, as a coach, for help:

"Please coach me in time management. I'm always late for everything."

At this very moment, his cell phone rang.

"Valery, I'm sorry, I totally forgot. I should have met you at 9 am today? I'm sorry. Can we do it tomorrow at 9? Okay then, thank you."

He hung up and turned back to me.

"David, why didn't you go to meet Valery today?" I asked.

"I forgot about our appointment."

"Did you not have it in your calendar?"

'No, because we made the appointment on the phone. I was on the go, and when I got to my office, I forgot to put it down."

"Is it possible that by the time you get back to your office today, you will have again forgotten about tomorrow's appointment?"

"Most likely. Unfortunately, I cannot use the digital calendar on my cell phone because of some compatibility issue."

"But if that compatibility issue were fixed, could you use your digital calendar on your mobile?"

"I think. I don't know, I'm not that much into mobile technology."

"You are running an IT company. You have 600 IT experts on your payroll. Do you think you can find one of them who can fix the compatibility issue?"

"Sure."

"Would you like to take action on this before our next meeting within two weeks?"

"Sure. But let's make it right now, not within two weeks. I want it so much, that I cannot wait another two weeks. Could you please drop me an email reminder so that I don't forget it by the time I get back to my office?"

CHAPTER 6
The Ugly Duckling

31

A ROLE MODEL INSTEAD
OF BEING LAME

A manager called me and said that he believed very strongly in coaching. During the previous four years, he had worked with four coaches, and all of them had done a great job. Each time they set a SMART goal, which have the following criteria:

- Specific – truly relevant to the coachee
- Measureable – can be represented by numbers
- Attractive – exciting enough to invest resources
- Relevant – possible to achieve
- Timely – achievable within a year.

He had achieved each of the goals he had set by the end of the year. But now he wanted something else. Something sustainable, to avoid having yet another coach, yet another goal. Something that he could only achieve over a longer period (over a year), and something that the closer he got to achieving, the happier he'd feel about it. He was deeply engrossed in talking about his life, relating a lot of specific examples. He explained that he and his family had been at the circus the day before. There was a clown, whose performance was kind of tasteless. But even worse, there was a woman sitting in front of him, laughing very loudly and slapping her thighs at the same time. He said she was so lame. At that time, I didn't really understand why he told me all this, and how it related to our coaching process.

We used "need cards" (special cards used in coaching processes which present different needs, like "I'd like to make the decision", "I'd like to have the responsibility", "I'd like to be recognized", etc.) We talked a lot about his dreams and aspirations from when he was younger. I went through all of the typical tools we use during such a process. We were sitting at the fourth or fifth session, when it was time to analyze role models. Who were his role models? When? Why these people? What were THEIR goals? And so on. All of a sudden, he slapped himself on the forehead and exclaimed, "How stupid I am! The woman I mentioned in our first session – well, at the time I thought she was so lame, but actually I really envied her. She is my role model! I want to laugh again instinctively, just like her!" Focusing on the word "again", we outlined a process together for how he could achieve long-term goals and not just one-year ones. We agreed that he would not need a coach and that he would simply enjoy the journey that leads him where he wants to be. As a parting gift, he gave me a ticket to see a stand-up comedy show. Sometimes he still calls me and tells me that he is doing fine and is following his own path.

32

A DREAM BEING LAUGHED AT

I am a person as well as a leader, and I have my own dream as well: I dream about the day when everybody will have a coach. Those who are not able to pay for it will be able to self-coach themselves. And I – as the ambassador of the SPARKLE self-coaching global CSR[21] program – will travel the world, pulling my suitcase with one hand and holding my husband's hand with the other, and give presentations about self-coaching at various locations around the world. The next day, we will take a sightseeing tour around the city and enjoy our time there; we'll gather new sources of inspiration and then return to our home afterwards. This will be a good way to give our kids some space, do something useful for the world and enjoy life while doing all of the above. We have always loved to travel, so this combination works well for both me and my family. When I first dreamed about this kind of life, we had just walked out of a theater after watching a performance of Mamma Mia, and I suddenly realized what my goal was with all my senses – my senses of hearing, sight, touch, smell and taste – exactly as we teach in the

21 Corporate Social Responsibility

VAKOG model (Visual, Auditory, Kinaesthetic, Olfactory, Gustatory). I was so overwhelmed with my own thoughts that I wrote all of it down in minute detail that night, right after we got home. The next day I read it to my team, and they all laughed. That was a very strong sign. A few months my team and I parted company, starting down different paths. I was forced to build a new team. It was not easy, but it was worth it. I may have been an ugly duckling, but I had finally found my swans.

Of course, it is important to make a profit, to make a company grow, and to bring the most out of ourselves, but the truth is, robots are also capable of doing the same thing. However, robots cannot have dreams. They are driven by something else. I am driven by my dream. Ever since then, I have known how important it is to surround myself with people who not only accept my dream, but also – if they can – support it. My new team and my own coach support me that way. I support my clients in the same way, because this is the only way I can stay authentic.

33

BEING "HOMESICK"

I was coaching the department head of a large IT company. He (like me) had studied and worked in the U.S., which meant that his social background was different from that of his colleagues. He had a cool style, he was self-confident and used conscious marketing to improve both his image of himself and that of his team. This behavior created the image of a selfish and superficial person in the minds of some of his colleagues. He was successful back in his homeland, but he felt as if an invisible glass dome had started to build up around his personality and that his chances of expanding his career were becoming more and more limited. Despite the fact that he had been working for this firm for more than a decade, and was successful and felt good about himself, something was still missing. He had this feeling that he had to suppress something deep inside of him – something that he thought was his strength, but which his environment considered to be the opposite. Like an ugly duckling.

During the diagnosis phase, as the coaching sessions turned into honest conversations, he finally was able to express his feelings: he wanted to work in an environment where his qualities were appreciated and were not something to suppress. From that point on, things accelerated and by the time our tenth coaching session rolled around, he had already received his work visa and was arranging a rental home for his family and a new school in Silicon Valley for his kids. Our original arrangement was to have ten coaching sessions, but he told me that he would very much appreciate it if we could add five additional sessions to the process, because he wanted me to support his integration process into the U.S. working environment. He considerately asked if the time difference would be a problem, because our sessions would start at 6 pm my time, after normal business hours in Europe. I told him that I always prefer to coach a sparkling-eyed manager after normal business hours than a faded one during normal business hours. He laughed and we made a schedule.

During our fifth session, he told me that people finally – including his boss and his colleagues – appreciated his valuable qualities, and things had turned out so well that he would be managing a subsidiary in Asia starting the following month – entailing a huge step forward in his career. I was happy to hear the good news. He retained those sparkling eyes and asked me whether I could still continue with the coaching sessions, but much earlier in the day (for me) this time? I said yes. For the ones with sparkling eyes – even outside of normal business hours – always.

34

DEMENTOR, DECOACH

I was coaching a director of a large company who told me that he enjoyed mentoring young people. Over the course of the previous four years, he had mentored four young professionals. Two out of the four were later promoted to a position that was higher than the mentor's own (one of them actually ended up becoming his boss), and the other two eventually left the company. Since all of this happened while the Harry Potter hype was at its peak, his colleagues came up with a new nickname they used for him from that point on: "Dementor". We talked about the conclusions to be drawn from this, the lessons learned, and things he should do differently in the future.

After this conversation, I thought about my own career while walking home. I did not want to pile pressure on my client by telling him my own stories, but if he was a "Dementor" then I was definitely a "Decoach". Within the previous year, I had coached 25 managers, but nine of them had left the country (they stayed with their companies but relocated to Switzerland, Denmark, Belgium, the Netherlands, the U.S., China, or elsewhere), while three of them got pregnant (as far as female top managers are concerned, by the way, this success rate outnumbers by far the success of any vitro fertilization program), and two of them had quit their jobs.

On those occasions when the coaching fee is paid by the company, I always raise a flag in advance to HR or the boss of the coachee that there is always a chance that the coachee might quit or, in the case of female coachees, end up having a baby. They always agree that, in such an event, whatever is better for the coachee will also be better for the company, enabling us to kick off the coaching process taking these outcomes into account. Whenever either one occurs, I always believe that it's better for the employer to not have a demotivated employee, and also for the employee to continue their career somewhere else.

In the latter two cases, the "blame" was to fall on our use of that handy coaching tool, the set of need cards.

Both times, I asked the coachees to select some cards from the 100 need cards: the ones that described their most important needs the best. Then I asked them to divide the cards they had selected into two categories, one in which the need should be fulfilled by their employer or colleagues, and another for which their family and friends were responsible. After they had done so, I asked them to divide the work-related cards into another two groups: the needs that were currently being fulfilled and the others that were not. In both cases, the piles in the latter category were way too large, and it didn't really matter what positive questions I asked, because the decision to be made seemed far too obvious. With these clear indications that they no longer wished to work for their current employers, I asked them to create a collage of their dream workplaces. Since they had already put their needs into words, visualization could further aid finding the right path. Their task was to look for attractive pictures in magazines and try to visualize the new workplace. It was interesting to find that each coachee had chosen a picture from a company that was a competitor to their current employer. Although both of them ended up remaining within their industries, one of them switched to another telecommunications company, while the other found a new job at a large competitor in the soft drink sector.

BASIC COMPUTER SKILLS

The majority of managers at least touch on the topic of time management within a coaching process. When this comes up, we discuss whether the manager uses some form of digital calendar and whether the manager's assistant or team has access to this calendar. In my experience, there are still very few managers who share their calendars with their colleagues.

My client wanted to restructure his organization and replace a number of employees, including his CIO. He was keeping a record of mistakes made and potential grounds for termination on his laptop. One day he decided that he wanted to show this file to me. His first idea was to print it out on a shared printer down the hallway. I asked him if he had any concerns that somebody else might pick it up before he did. He agreed that I had a point and said that I should look at the list on his laptop – and then he opened the file from a shared network drive. He didn't even know that it was possible to password-protect the document...

Ever since then, he has had his own printer in his office and if he has any confidential information to retain, he knows he can encrypt it. Quite useful to know, if you are about to fire an IT manager…

This reminded me of a saying:

"To err is human but to completely foul things up requires a computer."[22]

The story went on: although my client was not satisfied with the IT manager, firing him was not a viable option. Instead he asked me to speak personally with him in order to figure out whether there was anything that could be done about it. The IT manager was an introverted man, a bit taciturn. I felt he would not open up easily. I decided I would use a trick: in our next meeting, I pretended my laptop had suffered a fatal error. He was immediately up on his feet to fix it. He got so excited that he started explaining the nature of the problem at length: first, what the problem might have been and what could have caused it. Then he went on to say how much he loved fixing problems and how frustrated he was as a department head. I thanked him for his help, and he thanked me for the opportunity to help me – and he meant it. He had never wanted to be a department head. The previous director had put him in charge temporarily until a new manager could be recruited. But then the director left, and he end up remaining the department head. As he was not an

22 www.brainyquote.com/quotes/quotes/p/paulrehrl128388.html

assertive person, another reason why he would not make a good manager, he never communicated to the new director that he would rather go back to his old job.

When I was eighteen, I thought that everybody in the world wanted to become a manager – some made it and others didn't. Now I know it's not like that. This company now has a new IT manager, and the old one has returned to working as a system administrator – nobody was fired, and this way worked out the best for everyone.

36

DON'T READ TODAY'S PAPER!

The next story illustrates a quote from Nelson Mandela: "A critical, independent and investigative press is the lifeblood of any democracy."[23]

Most of my coachees work for multinational companies, but in this story, my client was the project manager for the largest project of a huge state-owned company. The management teams of state-owned companies usually come under closer scrutiny from the press than those of multinational companies. Here, the coaching process was aimed at supporting him during the last three months of the project, but with enormous risk: if the project was not concluded by the deadline, the company would suffer a million-dollar loss. The project manager had to cope with the stress while also delivering the project on time, and on budget.

And he did it. Afterwards, he went on a well-deserved vacation, and right on the day he returned to work, he called me:

23 At the International Press Institute Congress, 14 February, 1994

"Laura, don't read the local paper today!" He sounded very upset.

"Don't worry, I never do. What's in it?"

"Well, after the successful delivery of the project, I was promoted to head up the largest division in the company. I will be responsible for 950 employees. Many people don't like this. In today's paper there's an article saying I only got the job because my father was the CFO of the company, and that he was the one who helped me get this position. Since you are a business coach, we never discussed my private life. But I do want you to know that my father has been dead for 15 years, and had never even been to the city where I'm based. Also, he was an engineer, and never worked in finance. In light of all this, will you continue to coach me so that I can be a successful division head?"

"Sure. Same time, same place?"

37

STILL A GOOD MANAGER

My client was a mid-level manager at a large company. His supervisor, a director, asked me to coach this mid-level manager of his. But after only three sessions, the director called me to say, "Look, I know you cannot work miracles in just three sessions. I can see that you've started him off in the right direction. But I've made up my mind. I have been dissatisfied with his performance for years, so I am going to fire him. I would like to ask you to help him through this; so why don't you start working with him on finding a new job, figuring out what he would like to do next, and so on."

I wasn't happy to hear this. In fact, I felt horrible. I felt cheated. The director asked me to coach this manager in order for him to become a better manager. But now he had changed the name of the game. I felt as though I were now expected to say that he could not be developed into a better manager. I had sleepless nights.

I had had a number of executive clients before, and based on my experience, this manager wasn't doing that poorly at all. In fact, I thought it was the director, his supervisor, who was the one who could have been developed. It is surely not a sign of future-oriented leadership to hire a coach for your employee and then fire him three weeks later.

A few weeks passed, and the mid-level manager left the company with a nice severance package. The HR head called me afterwards:

"I'm really sorry about what happened to the mid-level manager and to you. You know, the director hasn't been a great leader; in fact, he was putting all the blame on his manager. Now the director is going to be terminated next month. I am calling you to ask you whether you would like to continue to work with your coachee, so that he will return to the company."

I was relieved that I had gotten the picture right. It was not my client who was to blame, but the director. I restarted the coaching process and my client returned to the company – this time as a director to replace his former boss.

CHAPTER 7

The Little Mermaid

38

AM I A GOOD MANAGER
BUT A BAD MOTHER?

When I first started working as a coach, I was a mother with a young child – just as many of my coaching clients are.

Coachee: "My daughter was one year old when I returned to work, because I didn't want to (and could not afford to) stay at home for longer. But now, when I'm sitting in boring meetings, I am constantly thinking how I would rather be home with her than sitting here wasting my time. Or at least I should be able to call her over the phone and speak with her."
  Coach: "And why don't you?"

This made her think. Ever since then, whenever she has started to feel that a meeting was not worthwhile, she has made it a habit to walk out of the room to call home and check on her daughter – who would have been around two years old then. This woman used to have a reputation for being a tough manager. Even though her behavior changed after she returned from maternity leave, she continued to be successful as a manager in her workplace. Maybe even more successful than before.

As John Maxwell said: "People will not give you their hand until they see your heart."[24] They saw her heart and reached out their hands.

While I was coaching several mothers who were returning to work after giving birth, clients who were planning on having a baby also started to ask me about this question. I was able to help them with insights and practical experience on how working mothers can succeed. Their typical question was this: "I want to have a baby, but what will happen to my job then?"

The majority of them eventually decided to seek a position to which they would be able to return easily after having a child, such as project management. When they proved to be successful after taking maternity leave, they often ended up in a higher position than they had been in before.

---

24 John C. Maxwell: *The 21 Irrefutable Laws of Leadership: Follow Them and People Will Follow You*, Thomas Nelson, 1998

39

OTHER PEOPLE'S DREAMS

Executive coaches are usually financed by the company; therefore, they have a right to have a say in selecting the goal of the coaching process. There are companies, however, that take advantage of this opportunity – meaning that either the manager of the client or an HR representative will provide their input during a joint session together with the coachee present. In the best-case scenario we leave room for setting up a realistic goal that the coachee wants to work toward and which fits the interests of his employer. It can also happen that the coachee feels "trapped" because he doesn't want to say "no" to the employer. In such cases, the coach must recognize what's happening and steer things in the right direction. In most cases, when I notice that the coachee is not quite comfortable with the selected goal, I ask his manager what efforts he plans to make in order to help the coachee achieve his goal. In my experience, there has never been a case where a manager did not want to answer this question. And since I am also witness to the conversation (for example, a promise is made that the coachee can make a speech or do a presentation in front of the board, or is authorized to practice speaking assertively with his manager at a conference, not just with his peers), in case the manager either reconsiders that maybe he set the bar too high for my coachee or he really becomes a committed supporter of the process.

But we have to be careful – not only with the coachee's manager – but also with some of the others who may indirectly influence the setting of the goal. On one occasion, I was coaching a successful female manager who told me that she liked to use visual tools, and prefers to also use them during the coaching process. As a result, she agreed to prepare a photo collage about her present and desired states, in order to aid the Situation and Positioning phases. I already became suspicious when she mentioned that she has only selected pictures that her husband also liked and envisioned situations in which her husband would also be happy. She said that her husband would be happy if he didn't have to work anymore and if he could take an afternoon nap in a hammock and had a vineyard and a wine cellar. However, she was nowhere in this vision. I asked her why. She replied, without thinking: *if my husband is happy, I am happy.*

I thought that if the process was so much influenced by the husband, that if he took part in the preparation (she may have asked him), then the coachee should do something else right here, during the session, when her husband was not present. Therefore I asked her to draw happiness and success curves. She prepared it quietly, and in an elaborate manner. When I asked her to tell me about the peaks in the curves, it turned out that all of them were finance-focused, such as her first pay raise, the first promotion, the first company car, and the Christmas bonus. Neither their honeymoon, nor the birth of their children was marked on the chart. Next, I asked, "Seeing these peaks, what could be the next happy moment in your life?" She instantly replied that it would be her promotion to be a board member. I asked her to tell me about a usual day of a board member, and explain how it would differ from her own daily activities. It turned out that she knew the names of only two out of the nine board members: the vice president and her own boss, but the other seven she didn't even know – therefore she couldn't tell how their life was different.

Obviously, it is not the duty of the coach to set the goal for the coachee. But there is a responsibility in examining how attractive the goal is, and what efforts can be made to achieve that goal. When it turned out that she wanted to be a board member in order to make more money so that she could buy the desired vineyard for her husband, so that he could spend more time there instead of annoying her and the children, it became a bit more clear what the real goal was and how the way to achieve it could be defined...

DEPUTY CEO WITH
EXTRA BAGGAGE

I was coaching a female deputy CEO who was the mother of two. I noticed during the very first session that she had many self-restricting beliefs, and I told her. I know this feeling very well and often catch myself trying to meet other people's expectations, but some of the things she said were way over the top.

She had been freshly promoted to a position in an industry where it was unimaginable to have a woman filling this role. She was the only woman in Europe to fill a position at this level. On one hand, this entailed a great acknowledgment of her ability, but on the other hand, she was suffering under a huge amount of pressure. She was responsible for the Finance Department (as she had been before), but now the HR, Legal and IT departments all fell under her responsibility. She did not hire a new finance manager to take on her previous duties, while the HR manager was still on maternity leave. The legal manager had left the firm for a competitor, so now she had to fill three managerial positions in addition to the previous one. She worked many hours overnight, but also wanted to be a perfect mom at home. She earned exactly ten times more than her husband, but felt ashamed when she did less housework then he did, saying, "A wife has to make sure that her home is tidy." She revealed another belief from her childhood: "Only a kept wife allows a cleaning lady to enter her home." Therefore she did not hire one. Moreover, she said that a child's school grades defined the quality of the mother, so she felt it was her responsibility to sit down with the child to do the homework and prepare for the next day's exam. And so on...

However, she could not stand up for herself in any of her roles, but rather suffered and played the role of a martyr. She told me that she was afraid to ask for very simple things, believing that it would be considered a nuisance. She preferred to pay for her own cell phone to replace the older model she had, because she felt uncomfortable during client meetings. The next day she noticed that all her colleagues were getting the same exact new cell phone from the company that she had bought for herself. In her free time, she paid for her own English classes, because her boss didn't speak any foreign languages; she was expected to improve her English to the level of proficiency of her French knowledge. She fought for other people's bonuses, but was afraid to ask for a pay increase in her new job, while receiving the same salary she earned when she was only managing the finance department.

She was full of honest complaints and went on and on talking about them after receiving permission from me to empty her mind. The classic coaching question of "Whose life are you living?" seemed a bit harsh at the moment, so first I started to build up some trust between us that could lead in the direction of change. We had a coaching session in the beginning of June. At the end of it I took out my calendar to schedule the date for the next session. I told her it would not be easy, because when school is out I spend four of the ten weeks with my kids (one week by the sea, another at Legoland, a third in Austria and the fourth at home), as well as another week with my husband in Brittany.

She did not say a word, but instead tears started rolling down her face. I gave her a tissue, and asked her what I had done to make her feel bad. She said nothing. It was simply the fact that she had not taken a total of five weeks of vacation in the past ten years altogether – ever since her elder child was born. Our attempt to schedule a date for our appointment was the last straw – as she later defined it – to finally convince herself that she really needed a change. Up until this point she thought that having a coach was only a "fancy hobby". During our next session, we worked with wisdom cards, and as fate had it, she drew a card – out of 100 cards – with a quote by Patricia Clafford: "Work can wait until you show the rainbow to your children. But the rainbow will not wait until you finish working."[25]

25 www.thequotablecoach.com/the-work-will-wait-while-you-show-the-child-the-rainbow/

She took a photo of the card and from that point on, the word "rainbow" became her mantra: whenever other people tried to detour her from her path. It became her password for the SAP system, for her mailbox, and at every possible location where she needed a reminder. Since then, she has hired a secretary, and her husband enjoys checking the children's math homework while she checks the French assignment (since it's a piece of cake for her) and she takes private English lessons together with her elder daughter. She sits at her computer after putting the kids to bed no more than once a week, and she has more private time, even time for an occasional massage – things that she could not have imagined before. The life of her husband has also changed: he has time to go bowling once a week with his friends, and the grandparents are also happy to help out with the kids.

Before our closing session, I received the following text message: "Today I took my elder daughter with me to the English teacher again. This is a win-win situation, because we both learn and our relationship gets stronger in the process. And imagine this: it was raining during the lesson, and as soon as we stepped outside we spotted a rainbow. We have been looking at it for some minutes, and I have tears of happiness in my eyes."

41

A SIGN OF GENEROSITY

A lot of newly promoted executives make the mistake of micro-management: they continue to supervise all operational details instead of focusing on true leadership issues. A newly promoted director at a multinational company was aware of this and asked me to help her in avoiding such mistakes. She specifically asked me to help improve her generosity and call her on it if she micro-manages.

We had our coaching sessions running for weeks, and as we were nearing the end, I compiled a summary of the process. Since she had a foreign boss, I put together my report in English. My client has a name ending in 's', which Microsoft Word spell checkers take for a plural noun. Therefore, all verbs in the report were automatically changed to the plural form – and I didn't realize it. I sent the report to my client first to review and she answered, "The report is fine. You can send it to my boss and issue your invoice. But there were several sentences where you wrote 'have' instead of 'has'." I thanked her for the reply and made a comment: "Maybe you shouldn't pay the invoice, as I apparently didn't do a good enough job with you."

Within a few hours, a very generous gift package was delivered to my door. It was from my client, with a card: "Thank you for everything. I know I still have a long way to go but I hope you will see I have improved in generosity."

As Ken Blanchard put it: "To form an attractive vision is the privilege of executives but it is their biggest challenge as well."[26]

There are executives who remain unable to paint an attractive picture of the future until they stop wasting their time and energy on micro-management.

26 www.goodreads.com/author/quotes/4112157.Kenneth_H_Blanchard

42

BORDER-CROSSING GOALS

As the name of our company indicates (Business Coach Ltd), our clients come mainly from the business field, and usually bring business topics to the coaching sessions. We always inform them that we essentially coach humans who actually happen to be managers, but if clients feel like bringing up a topic that involves their private life, that's not a problem either. We are not here to investigate anybody's private life, so the clients can share as much as they think is necessary to help achieving their business goals. At times the clients realize that they follow the same patterns at home that they do at the workplace, and other times they try to implement a change in one area, and if it works, they implement it in the other as well. Some of them are parents and managers at the same time, and notice that they are stronger in one role and aim to implement this well-functioning attitude in the other role as well. One example is a person who did a very good job of recruiting and training his successor at the workplace, while his son was still wearing Velcro shoes, because he was not able to learn how to tie them properly. Or, it could work the other way: someone who was very strict at home about how much time the kids were allowed to play with their

X-boxes or Minecraft had to face the fact that the employees were spending more time on Facebook than actually working. These are always fine examples, and the coachees are able to benefit from the well-functioning solutions and implement them in other situations.

So when a coaching process is aimed at business life, but personal relevance is also discovered: we solve both. However, when a client approaches us with strictly personal topics, we always inform them that we can help, but we have sufficiently less experience in private matters, and a life coach is usually cheaper than a business coach. Once there was a client who did not accept this reasoning. He was a top manager at a large bank, and I had coached him a few years earlier. The process was successful, he achieved his goal, but just before Christmas, he called me on my mobile. I thought he wanted to wish me a Merry Christmas, but this was not the case. He told me that his wife had just had a baby (we didn't talk about personal matters during the sessions, I wasn't even aware that he had a family) and, unless I accepted the challenge to be his life coach, he was not going to spend Christmas with his family any longer. Now I know that it was a big mistake to accept the challenge. I was very much moved by the process, so I was attending supervision in parallel to it. I don't know what I would do if something like this happened again, but I know that if I listened to my head, I'd definitely refer the client to someone else.

43

TEARS FOR A PULLOVER

Some coaches specialize in self-branding or styling. I am not one of them, but at times I still come across client cases like this one: Once I met a newly promoted female director who wore a very skimpy miniskirt and a sexy top for our first appointment. The outfit suited her perfectly and made quite an impression on everyone around her. She was a very pretty lady, no doubt. I made an innocent comment about how she must have had an easy day at the office, since she was able to stop by her apartment to change for today's party before meeting me. It turned out she had come straight from her office. She got the message, and for our next appointment she was dressed in proper business attire.

At another company, the new board member was looking for a coach who would be upfront and honest with her under any circumstances. I met her, and we both felt the chemistry, but she really wanted to test straightforward communication. She asked me to give her developmental feedback based upon our very first meeting.

Coach: I'm in quite a difficult situation here; it is really hard to identify an area for improvement based on one single meeting. You have not said anything that would really strike me as an area of concern. But if you accept it, I would offer a comment on your image: you could work on looking more professional.

Coachee: What do you mean?

Coach: I mean I've never been in a board member's office stuffed with cuddly teddy bears. Or met a board member who was using a cheap, disposable pen to make notes in a student notebook. And the photo you have on the wall there, with you standing among the other board members wearing a pullover. Everyone else is in a suit and tie.

Coachee: But that was a very expensive pullover! And very trendy. I bought it recently to wear for the board photo. Maybe we have different tastes in dressing.

Coach: I'm not saying I don't like your pullover. I'm saying what you can see in the picture: everyone else is wearing a suit and tie.

Coachee: I don't want to talk about this issue. This will not make me a better leader. I don't need a coach to criticize my pullover.

Coach: Well, okay, I'm sorry. I didn't want to criticize you, you asked me to give you developmental feedback. If you expected me to find no area for development, if you want a coach to praise you, then I'm not your man. Good luck and goodbye!

I left, and the assistant walked me to the elevator. As I looked back, I could see a tear in the board member's eye. I was sitting in the cab, thinking. What was this all about? Did I really hurt her so badly? Maybe I should not have picked on anything. But she was testing my honesty...

I felt regretful about this, because the meeting before I made my comment had gone great. I thought we could really work together. Then my phone rang:

Coachee: "You passed the test. I want an honest coach like you. Let's meet next week!"

44

A COLORLESS LEADER

Once I coached a female manager who was often interviewed on television. She had participated in a special media training course to improve her public speaking. The training course was run by well-known and popular media personalities who interviewed her with embarrassing questions while the cameras were filming. Then she could watch the video and see how she turned red with embarrassment or got upset. They analyzed in detail what went well and what could be improved. She received a lot of good advice, as well as a comment that she could not deal with. This became the topic for our next coaching session. The comment was that she was "colorless": uninteresting in what she says and how she says it. She did not attract attention via her presented topic or via her presentation style.

In our coaching session, we brainstormed ideas on both the "what" and "how" of presenting. As for how, that night she read a bedtime story to her son. Then she recited the story in her own words, in a colorful way. Her son was so impressed, he didn't even recognize it was the same story. The manager now had immediate feedback on how she could multiply the effect of her presentation with a different style – even if it requires slightly more energy. So she tried it the next week in a company presentation: she rehearsed it in front of a mirror at home before, but it was worth the time. It went great!

As for the "what" to say, she had more work to do on this. She had been a "high-flyer" ever since her childhood: always the first in class, always meeting all expectations. She was quickly promoted to a high position at work and wanted to prove herself. She didn't even realize she was trying to live up to somebody else's dreams rather than her own. She never stopped work for an extended holiday or to take time for adventures. She worked like a robot, in a steady, dull way. All of her life was dull and colorless. And she was not ready to change this all at once – just for the sake of improving her presentation skills. She did make a small step, though:

At her office, dozens of local and English business papers appeared every week. She had been reading them for years, and read nothing else but these. But for a change, she walked to the nearest newsstand and picked up some magazines she had never bought. Not tabloids with unpleasant stories, but rather high-quality magazines about history, gastronomy, lifestyle, home design and so on. She flipped through them and picked an article from each that she could use in her next company presentation. She had great success with her colorful presentations and was reassured that this was the way forward.

Ever since then she has not only subscribed to new magazines, but also signed up for a cooking course and started ballroom dancing – living a colorful life that is not only for giving colorful presentations.

CHAPTER 8

The Steadfast
Tin Soldier

EQ=0

I have had a number of clients with a very high IQ who also had, at the same time, a very low EQ – emotional quotient. A CEO called me once that he was in search for a coach for his sales manager to improve his EQ. The CEO explained the situation and set an objective, and I subsequently met the sales manager for an introductory meeting.

The CEO expected the sales manager to spend more of his time out in the field, talking to the sales reps. He was spending too much time in his office and missing out on a lot of valuable market information, the CEO said. The sales manager gave a similar description of the issue:

"Look, Laura, I have a very low EQ, maybe even negative. I don't go out into the field because I'm not interested in those people: I don't care how they feel, what they want, I just want them to do their jobs."

He talked at length about how he was not a social person, but was more of an egoist, and the only things he cared about meeting were his sales objectives. During his 15-minute self-description, he asked me twice if

I wanted another cup of tea whether I was cold, or if he was speaking too fast. I felt some incongruence and decided to hold up a mirror to him:

"You said you don't care about people's feelings. And yet, you met me only 15 minutes ago and have been very caring toward me. How is that?"

He started thinking. He said he was a loyal company man and he really respected his boss. When the boss said he didn't care about people, he didn't want to disagree.

His father had been a career soldier, and he never went against his father's wishes.

The sales manager was a very loyal person indeed, not just at work but also in his family setting. He would do all he could to please others. As his family loved living out in the country and did not want to move into a big city, he decided to commute to work: five hours of driving back and forth every day. It also showed me a man with high EQ, who truly cared about the needs and feelings of others.

I started digging deeper, so that we wouldn't try to fix a problem that didn't exist. I asked him to count out all the reasons why he really didn't spend time out in the field. It turned out most of them were connected to a lack of time.

For the next coaching session, I asked him to put together a list of activities he does routinely every week, their duration, and identify which ones could be eliminated or delegated. With a few simple shortcuts, he could re-organize his weekly appointments so that he would not have to drive into the city on one out of the five workdays the next week, thus saving five hours of driving. That day he could spend working on strategic issues. Then he was able to free up another day during the week, which he used to go out in the field to meet with the sales representatives.

He arrived at our fourth coaching session with a big smile and a comment about how sorry he was to not speak with his sales representatives earlier. He learned a lot about them and collected lots of ideas, which they have already started to implement. He discovered that he did in fact care for people, their feelings and their goals. And as he got to know them better, he now understood how he could best support them. They really made a great team together.

46

27 ALTERNATIVES
WITH STORY CUBES

The Story Cube is a simple die, like dice used in gaming that can be purchased at any toy store. The only difference is that this one has basic pictures on it, instead of the usual dots.

We usually bring in the cube at the Alternative collection phase of the SPARKLE model, when the coachee "cannot see the forest for the trees" and is only capable of seeing one or two options in a decision-making situation.

I was coaching the expatriate vice-president of a pharmaceutical company. The process was going forward nicely, but one time he was fuming when he came to the session and told me he was about to turn in his resignation immediately, and the only thing he was sorry about was the fact that our coaching sessions would therefore also come to an end. I recalled that previously he had mentioned that if he were to stay with this company in his position in Hungary until April 1, (meaning he did not "run away"), then he would get a substantial bonus, namely 100,000 euros, because in previous years, none of his predecessors had been able to stay out the one-year term. I asked him whether this offer was still valid, meaning he only had to stay 13 more days, out of which four were weekend days, thus adding up to only nine working days. He said yes, it was, and smiled as he quickly calculated how many euros each additional day would be worth. But this smile wasn't really a remedy for his fury, and he asked me – since he was already here – if I would be kind enough to listen to him and let him cry out his pain. He told me that we didn't need to find a solution, he really did not have any expectations, he just wanted to tell me the story because there was no one else he could tell this to.

He talked about his problem, I listened, then summarized what I had heard. I tried not to reduce the importance of the problem, because I knew that this would only add fuel to the fire; while he was talking and listening to my summary his fury seemed to ease. Then he asked me if we could assess the situation and maybe find an alternative solution in order to avoid his immediate resignation.

Lot of coaches carry many tools that can aid in finding alternatives, and a coach can always freely choose the best one that fits the client's personality or the challenge. As we all know, most women have many handbags. This morning I took a handbag with me that I had not used since the previous December. There was also a box of story cubes with our logo printed on it in them left over from the past Christmas, as we had given it out to customers as a Christmas gift. It was probably not a coincidence that this was hiding in my bag. I took it out and explained how we use it in the coaching process. We usually play a game in which the coachee was asked to roll the nine cubes individually and come up with an alternative solution inspired by the pictures on the cubes. He laughed (this was another good sign of his mood lightening up) and told me that this would be impossible. He could not possibly come up with nine alternatives to solve the situation.

A bit later, he got so into the game that he came up not with nine solutions, but 27 altogether; meaning he actually rolled each die three times. There were some "harsh" solutions, such as waiting for his boss in the parking lot and beating him up right there. And there were funny ones too; for example, he would draw a smiley face on a paper bag and pull it over his head for the remaining nine days, but at the end, out of the 27, he was able to select a feasible solution that he felt he could work with.

He got his bonus, went on a nice long holiday (more than nine days), had a chance to relax and evaluate his situation, then went on achieving a goal based on an idea he got from the cubes (it was a recycling sign), and now he is the vice president of the company. He still recalls that if it hadn't been for those magic cubes, he might not be living in the beautiful city of Budapest any longer, nor would he be working for his current company...

47

THIS IS NOT COACHING: CFO WITH A DEGREE IN LITERATURE

There is an endless debate on whether a coach should have relevant industry experience and/or leadership experience. Before I became a coach, I had worked as a management consultant, where relevant experience had always been high on the clients' list of selection criteria. And sometimes it is really tough for me as a coach to refrain from giving advice based on my experience.

A few years ago, I had the privilege of presenting at an international coach conference. Sir John Whitmore, the godfather of coaching, was the keynote speaker, and my presentation came just after his. I followed him out during the break, and we had a chance to talk. I shared with him the challenge I was facing, that of having worked as a management consultant before becoming a coach, and in that earlier role it had been expected of me to share the best practice, to give advice, to have the Sorcerer's Stone. Now that I was a coach, it was not easy for me to not give advice. He, as one of my role models, answered with the following: "I am really happy if I give advice to my coachees only 20 percent of the time."

So I hope the case below will also be considered to be a non-fatal error in judgement of a junior coach who wanted to help her client more than anything.

One of my clients was the head of the legal department. His work was much appreciated, and he was promoted to chief operating officer. It was well known within the company that he had no business background; in fact, he had a teaching degree. He was put in charge of a very competent team: they could deliver the results almost by themselves. What they really needed was a true leader.

As I have a master's degree in economics, I could help my client quickly understand the basics of finance and accounting. At least to the extent that he could recognize a balance sheet and a profit and loss account and know if he should be happy or worried if the numbers were getting higher or lower on a specific line. Clearly, relevant expertise was a great asset for me as a coach in this case.

Coaches can also help their clients a lot without relevant experience: by researching, reading and extracting related articles. In such cases the coach is a kind of "hired reader", which can be also useful for the coachee if this is required.

At the end of the coaching process, I thought it appropriate to present my client with the book *The Daily Drucker*[27]. He, too, had picked a surprise gift for me: a calendar with poems. For the next year, he had a quote from a management guru for each day, and I had a verse.

27 Peter F. Drucker: *The Daily Drucker*, HarperCollins, 2004

48

A VERY EXPENSIVE FRIEND

My coachee was promoted to a regional leadership position at a multinational company. His former colleague and friend had put a "congratulations" card on his desk in his new office, in a new office building. The client was touched, and still was when he told the story to me as his coach. But when I asked him how he had acknowledged this gesture, he replied shyly "I didn't." Two weeks had passed since receiving the card.

The client made a promise to thank his friend for the card personally before our next coaching session, no matter how busy he was. We met less than two weeks later.

Coach: How are you feeling today?
Coachee: Horrible.
Coach: Why?
Coachee: Because I miss my friend. We used to go out to lunch every day and talk.
Coach: And why don't you keep doing it now?
Coachee: Because my friend thinks I would be lowering myself by meeting him.
Coach: Why does he think so?

Coachee: Because I haven't called him since I moved office. I haven't even thanked him for the card.

Coach: Why?

Coachee: It's not because I didn't have the time. I know it's not an excuse, I could always free up five minutes. But I felt so awkward, calling him after two weeks, and now after four weeks...

Coach: Do you still want to meet him? Do you want to continue to be his friend?

Coachee: Yes.

Coach: Want to call him now?

Coachee: No.

Coach: Do you want to take this again as your homework from today's coaching session?

Coachee: Yes.

Coach: Will you call him then in the next two weeks?

Coachee: No.

Coach: Do you want to continue feeling frustrated for the next two weeks?

Coachee: No.

Coach: Want to call him now?

Coachee: No.

Coach: If you were him, would you be angry?

Coachee: Yes.

Coach: If you were him, would you forgive him if you finally called to say thank you after four weeks?

Coachee: Yes.

Coach: Want to call him now?

Coachee: He won't answer the phone, because he knows my number.

Coach: Want to use my phone then?

Coachee: Yes.

So he did. I ended up with a high phone bill as they talked at length, but a friendship was saved – which is worth every penny for managers in top positions.

49

DON'T YOU WANT TO BE
OUR VICE PRESIDENT?

One of my coachees was working directly for the vice president. He contacted me with the goal of improving his communication skills. Whenever a coachee starts off with such a common goal (the other most popular is "how to become a better leader"), then we always have to dig a bit deeper to specify how exactly they want to improve. What does better communication mean to you? With whom do you want to communicate better? About what, when and how? When we began to peel the onion, it turned out that he had also been a manager in several other countries and had always been able to cooperate with his colleagues. He was also doing well in his current job, except for one thing: he could not get along well with the vice president. We assessed that they actually got along well when discussing daily operational tasks, but when it came to strategic decisions, he had a sense of not being understood. We assessed the methods that one could use to explain something to the other. He brought several examples of how he had explained things in the past to other people. He told me how he helped his son understand things, and how they sometimes took things apart to help his son understand how things work. As another example, one of his previous subordinates was a visual type, and therefore he had a large whiteboard in the office with colorful markers where he used to draw a picture of his ideas. With people who could be convinced by expert opinions, he brought in some books on the topic. When he wanted to discuss long-term plans with his wife, instead of dropping ideas during the morning rush, he took her to a spa in order to relax and talked about his plans while having a nice dinner. There were many examples he could recall, and he raised several great ideas on the topic.

He implemented all of these ideas in practice and every week he tried a different approach with the vice president. He drew a picture, invited him to lunch, brought up real-life examples and instead of suggesting a book (because he was well aware that the VP would not take the time to read it) he sent him a short, 12-minute TEDx video. At each coaching session, he told me what he did and how it had absolutely no effect. We were at the sixth or seventh session when he asked me to take part in an experiment. I am only a coach, and I knew nothing about his industry, but he wanted to explain his strategy to me and see if I was able to understand it. He brought in a short video, some colorful markers, a two-page best practice article and started to explain his thoughts. I asked a lot of questions, but within a short time I understood it. He paused and quietly took a few minutes to think, then asked me, "Don't you want to be our Vice President?" I smiled and said that I love being a coach, and I'd love to help him reach his goal. I asked him to define his goal again. His goal was not to make sure that the VP understood him, but to work for a boss who was able to understand him.

He listed the alternatives for his new goal. He could either go back to a country where he worked previously or stay in Hungary, but find another company to work for. But there was a third option as well. The international directors were experiencing some problems with the current VP, who was unable to understand the corporate goals. It turned out that the VP was not capable of fulfilling the expectations for his position. He was soon sent to another country to work on an "operational" role. My coachee was able to prove his abilities. It turned out that I was not elected to be the new VP, but I did, however, remain the coach of the new VP.

50

GOOD TIMES, BAD TIMES /
WE LAUGH TOGETHER,
WE CRY TOGETHER

A business journalist called me to tell me that he was interviewing market players who could increase their turnover in spite of the global economic crisis. Coaches are indeed amongst those who benefited from the economic downturn, as many corporate executives needed support in facing issues they had never had to face before, like standing up in front of 500 employees to announce a major downsizing.

I met a CEO who decided he wanted to make the best that he possibly could out of the crisis. Not only financially for the company, but also in strengthening his leadership skills and image. In terms of turnover, his company's was one of the biggest in the country, ranging between fifth and tenth in the national rankings each year, and he wanted to put it in the top three. This was a challenging goal, and I felt really excited about the process.

During our first two coaching sessions, I felt he was keeping something back. Then I used a trick to make him show his cards. Apparently, he had made some bad mistakes in communicating the company's restructuring earlier. Now more downsizing was on the way, and this time he wanted to do it the right way.

I could feel his anxiety; his eyes showing signs of regret. He shared that on the day of the first restructuring announcement, his new company car finally arrived – a limousine he had ordered before the crisis struck. So he drove the brand new limo to the manufacturing site, which was out of town. The factory workers were so upset by the limo that they almost mobbed him.

I asked him what he would do differently this time. He said he would definitely not drive a limo, he would take a train instead.

   "And what else would you do differently?"
   "I would not wear a suit and tie. I'd rather wear the standard factory uniform so that they could see I'm one of them, not just some big shot from the headquarters. My slogan would be: 'We share in good times, we share in bad times'."
   "And what else?"

He brainstormed a lot of ideas. He developed a very detailed game plan for the next Big Day. I crossed my fingers for him and really hoped that he would not get physically hurt by egg-throwing or similar tactics as he announced another major layoff. He didn't call me all day and all night, so I called him the next morning in despair: "Are you still alive?"

"Sure! It was cold and raining but I still took the train and the factory uniform. They got the message. Imagine, we've come up with the idea that we will not lay off a hundred workers but reduce the directors' and my salary so that we can keep the workers employed for half-time at least. You know, being the only employer in the region, this is a big thing. And I didn't call you last night because I ended up staying really late with them. By the time we brainstormed all the ideas, I had missed the last train. So I stayed over at the workers' hostel, and we talked until dawn. Now they all believe our company will survive the crisis and even become the market leader! And then we will again share in good times!"

RECOMMENDATIONS

Being a leader who believes in the power of organizational development, putting coaching mentality into the core of it is the best thing one can do. Employees will start to own their problems, their solutions, their results. If you share this belief, this book with practical advices, stories, tools is a must- have for you.

Zoltan Radeczky, Regional General Manager, AVON

This highly readable and enjoyable book provides brilliant insights about coaching and leadership. Laura Komocsin shares 50 powerful stories that bring coaching concepts to life and inspire any leader in order to better connect with people at all levels.

Patrick Stapfer, Regional Managing Director, CRH

Great read not only for coaches but for anyone in or contemplating being in a coaching relationship in any country. Laura's style is down to earth, with a gentle humour that will spark contemplation and enthusiasm in the same measure.

Graham O'Mahoney, Regional Director, Provident

As an HR executive, I could easily relate to many of the stories because I have either experienced similar situations or there is a good chance that the others might happen to me any time. I really appreciate that it not only contains success stories, but also some examples of when the process has failed.

Veselina Petrova, HR director, Deichmann

Being already for many years in different management positions, I have to say that several of the stories in the book seemed familiar to me. I really liked the practical, real-life experience that came through the stories. The book is a joy to read for every leader. I myself read it in one go.

Frank Van de Vel, Senior Managing Director, KBC Group

I love the idea of this book: to develop through tales, to bring in new perspectives for old situations. The characters and stories in Andersen's tales can be related to new business concepts and make them easier to comprehend and remember. I recommend this book to all who are responsible for developing people. A truly creative way to expand your managerial toolkit.

Attila Keszeg, VP Europe, Deutsche Telekom

Great coaching anecdotes that both educate and amuse.

Stuart McAlister, MD, Inter Relocation Group

Such a refreshing book! There are so many coaching books on the market saying the same thing, in the same way, just by different authors. Laura takes a truly creative approach that is both original and engaging. These 50 stories are far from fairy tales, these are real examples from a skilled and passionate coach.

Ian Day, co-author of *Challenging Coaching*

This book is a fast-pace, inspiring journey through the many adventures of leadership coaching. With entertaining stories, witty observations and useful references, Laura guides us on this journey with an expert's experienced eye. The book imaginatively opens our eyes to the magic of coaching from which we can learn how to become better coaches and leaders.

John Blakey, author of *The Trusted Executive*

Business Coach Ltd.
Responsible publisher: Laura Komócsin PCC

Layout, prepress: Layout Factory Grafikai Stúdió

ISBN 978-963-12-7002-0

Printed by: Amazon